DR. JEFFREY MAGEE

CMC/CBE/PDM/CSP

ACHIEVEMENT

DEI of

TALENTification!

The 11-Elements to Execution and ACHIEVEMENT of the
DEI Talent Management Model for a Healthy, Sustained
& Engaged Organization!

DEI-Of-TALENTification

Second Edition

ISBN: 979-8-9892760-1-1

US $44.99

Copyright 2020/2024 Business/Management/Leadership/Human Potential/Organizational Development

Magee, Jeffrey L., PhD/CMC/CBE/PDM/CSP

DEI-of-TALENTification The 11-Elements to Execution and ACHIEVEMENT ™ of the DEI Talent Management Model for a Healthy, Sustained & Engaged Organization

Green, Sheryl, editor

Wittenwiler, Taryn, copy editor

Alem Sacak, cover design editor

Performance 360 Media Group / Jeffrey Magee, LLC, publisher

Performance 360 Media Group Las Vegas, Nevada

www.jeffreymagee.com

A New Era in Publishing™

For information regarding special discounts for bulk purchases for business training emersion, large groups, personalized edition for your group, families and gifts, please contact the following:

Las Vegas, Nevada

www.JeffreyMagee.com

DEI-Of TALENTification™ Endorsements

"Unlock your potential by following the inspiring and powerful advice in this book. By understanding you have the ability to control your destiny, the possibilities become endless!"

Dr. Nido Qubein
President, High Point University
Chairman, Great Harvest Bread Co.

Dear Jeffrey,

Thank you so much for submitting your capstone project. I have to say that this is very impressive. It was therefore such a pleasure to read it and it really inspired me. I wish we had more time to discuss all your excellent points and reflections.

So, with the limitations of time and space, I would just really like to highlight some of the aspects of your capstone project that really impressed me. I really liked your thoughts on TALENTification.

As we discussed so many times during the Office Hour: Culture eats strategy for breakfast (and you also quoted Peter Drucker, which is wonderful) and if you do not have the buy-in of your employees and overlook their fears and worries, the best DEI strategy will not stick. Great that you included such strong points on developing a clear data strategy. DEI has influences on the bottom line and should be displayed just like we show financial analysis. You demonstrated your deep understanding of DEI, as you also pointed to ongoing DEI initiatives such as implementing and communicating the organizations DEI talent strategy, establishing the governance structure and empowering diversity leaders.

The Japanese principle Kaizen - change for the better or continuous improvement - comes to mind. Just like gardening, we need to continuously speak and reflect together on the effects of our implemented DEI initiatives. This is an evolution and not a revolution.

Well done and I hope you will implement this strategy and make the world a more inclusive place. It has been a pleasure having you on the course and I wish you all the best for your future and hope our paths will cross again. Warm wishes, Laura

Dr. Laura Wuensch
University Of Cambridge, Judge School Of Business,
Executive Education
Administrator/Instructor

"Your every action and interaction influence where you go in life. In Jeff's new book, TALENTification, the steps to taking control of your personal and professional pathways for success are detailed for easy understanding and, more importantly, application. In my life and in my business, I have learned first person that success leaves clues and mistakes add up; this book gives you clear vision for the trajectory that leads to greatness in talent management."

Frank W. Abagnale
FBI Special Agent, Subject of the book, movie and Broadway musical,
Catch Me If You Can

"Dr. Magee's advice and counsel is always right on target. This book will help you identify your trajectory and lead a more effective and satisfying life."

Kathy Taylor, Esq.
Dean, The University of Tulsa: Collins College of Business
Former Secretary of State Oklahoma,
Mayor Tulsa Oklahoma,
Harvard Fellow
Board Member, SONIC Restaurant

"Trajectory Code Diagram and the Player Capability Index – These are the tools that I use at employee reviews and to challenge people to come up with their personal goals. This is my favorite of Dr. Magee's models. TALENTification takes the understanding and discussion of talent management to levels that have immediate and lasting impact on the health of an organization!"

Aaron Johnson, CEO
Farm Credit Illinois
$6 Billion in Holdings

"As a leader of Soldiers for over 30 years, talent development is not a new topic … A fresh perspective and approach, is always appreciated. Dr. Magee's high-energy presentation is exactly that fresh approach to give our Soldiers something new for their toolbox."

"Dr. Magee's approach to leadership focuses on the little things; the seemingly-minute details that can be the difference between winning and losing on the battlefield. His seminar left the senior leaders of our organization with a lot to think about, and a brand-new perspective on how to get the job done."

Evon, Francis J Jr MG USARMY NG CTARNG (US)
Adjutant General, Connecticut National GUARD

"I've known Jeff for over 15 years and he has always over delivered. As my friend, Joel Weldon would say, 'He promises much -- and delivers more.'"

Bob Pike, CSP/CPAE/CPLP Fellow
Chairman/Founder – Training and Performance Forum
ASTD/ATD Icon

"When I served as CEO of the National FFA Organization, Dr. Jeff worked with the National FFA Alumni in helping us redefine our focus and strategy going forward. His enthusiastic and professional approach was well received by our alumni leadership and by our membership. Jeff worked with our management team and also served as the key facilitator in a large conference setting. His keen ability to relate to his audience and engage everyone was demonstrated in both of these groups. Jeff is one of the best in the business in his presentation skills, but his follow-up is phenomenal. He is a great listener and his people skills are outstanding. Jeff is a quick learner and he works hard to fully understand his customer and is very straightforward with honest assessment and recommendations. You should not hesitate to contact Dr. Jeff for your next project, regardless of the size of your project. He will exceed your expectations."

Dr. Dwight Armstrong, former CEO
FFA Organization

"Dr. Jeff is a giver that over delivers. I have personally learned from his business brilliance and have been blessed by his generosity."

David Horsager, CSP
Author, Speaker, Consultant
TRUST Edge Leadership Institute

"Jeff is a common-sense guru who goes beyond theory to practical ideas that work to increase revenue and profit. He is insightful, clear and extremely relevant to any organization wanting to compete at an elevated level."

Roxanne Emmerich, CSP/CPAE
Founder at Institute for Extraordinary Banking

"I first met Jeff many years (25+) ago and was very impressed with his insights into performance and his incredible communications abilities. So, I retained him to help me motivate and build teamwork talent within my team at Target Corporation. Needless to say, he significantly exceeded that expectation and he has provided me with wisdom and guidance ever since then.

I recommend Dr. Jeff Magee highly for his professionalism, his insight into people and his motivational and communications capabilities. While there are quite a few good motivational speakers out there, very few, if any, achieve the outstanding results Jeff brings to an organization."

King Rogers
Former SVP TARGET/Sr. Assets Protection Advisor

"Jeff is a high-class entrepreneur, expert, and developer of people and organizations. I'm happy to recommend him as a coach, consultant, and/or trusted advisor."

Alan Weiss,
Author of Million Dollar Consulting and Thrive: Stop Wishing Your Life Away; *Best Selling Author of* The Million Dollar Maverick at Summit Consulting

"Talent Development: I had the opportunity to spend 1 ½ days learning from Dr. Magee at the National Association of Electrical

Distributors Sales Management Bootcamp in Austin, TX, and also during the 4-hour Strategic Leadership workshop he presented at the NAED LEAD Conference in Denver, CO, in July 2017. Dr. Jeff's innovative and rapid-fire delivery of leadership & sales strategies and techniques taught us all many new skills that could be immediately applied in our businesses and will no doubt positively impact our companies and careers for years to come. I have attended many personal and professional development educational conferences and workshops over my 27-year career and Dr. Magee is the best of the best. His real-world experience, outstanding educational credentials and expert mastery of his subjects, combined with an enthusiastic, engaging delivery style and his passion for guiding others to success, makes attending one of his educational sessions feel like you're sitting in a College Master's Degree Level course."

Vito DiMaio,

Director of Marketing & Employee Development at Stoneway Electric Supply

"I am pleased to write this letter of recommendation for Dr. Jeff Magee. I've known Dr. Magee for about four years on a professional and personal level and believe that he is one of the most dynamic and well-versed professional leaders in the industry of human-capital investment.

As the Deputy Adjutant General for the Vermont National Guard, Dr. Magee has improved the dignity and respect received by the soldiers and airmen with whom he works. He became part of the training resources for our recruiting force program by making key strides to the strategic view. He took his program and ultimately integrated it into the recruiting mission to meet our strength goal. He leads the way in quality of work and the ability to relate and communicate with senior-level officials. His competence, drive, and outstanding performance of duty continue to set the example for others to follow.

Dr. Magee has conducted numerous presentations in recent years and has always exhibited exceptional competence and incredible professionalism that would benefit any organization. He conducts his leadership training and recruiting methods on the C-Suite level and down to the most junior soldier with integrity and superior performance, all driven by his personal motivation for success. Dr. Magee has the unique ability to transfer this energy to the commands and to the successes of organizations with whom he works.

It is my opinion that Dr. Jeff Magee will enhance your organization with balance, integrity and teamwork. There are no limits: his leadership and human-capital development will greatly contribute to the success of your organization."
BG Michael Heston (Ret.)
Deputy Adjutant General, Vermont National Guard

Contents

DEI-of-TALENTification

The 11 Elements to Execution and ACHIEVEMENT of the DEI Talent-Management Model for a Healthy, Sustained & Engaged Organization!

Values, Grace, Dignity, Self-Respect and Adherence to the Law transcends all DIVERSITY ... And, everyone owns holding those fully accountable that would defile any factor that creates a stereotype that brings us all down!

Introduction

DEI, here we go again. I can already hear the voices in most people's head when the term DEI is mentioned. However, if you stop and reflect for a moment, it is what every child is taught, don't judge, be accepting and learn how to see other people for who they are and get along with them. Let everyone have an opportunity, share your toys, be nice, if you can't say something nice, don't say anything at all.

It is only as we get older that we begin to be conditioned to shut down and have our biases towards diversity, inclusion and letting others have their opportunity.

So, give it any "name" you would like if DEI bothers you. And given that the concept of TALENTification should really just be about great human kind endeavors, the concept of Diversity may also be inclusive of accessibility as well.

So, maybe every time you hear, read or say DEI, as this is the global accepted and embedded business and sociological term, maybe it should really be around **DEI(A) – Diversity, Equity, Inclusion and Accessibility.**

It is from the diversity of thoughts and ideas that the greatest outcomes can be experienced and the greatest of challenges can be resolved. The greatest outcomes can be realized when you have aligned diversity of individuals with a shared VALUE system and goals.

Alignment of all capital assets drives organizational effectiveness and success, and human capital talent at every level is the most critical asset from which everything in an organization is derived.

The people that you align yourself to and the people that work within your organization, are the only market differentials in tomorrow's market space. Whatever other assets you have, the competition can acquire and what ever assets the competition has, you can acquire – it is a zero net market and the reality of relevance is your human capital equation.

The pivot point or trajectory recalibration for human-capital success is the art and science of crafting an indelible culture and organization that allows you to recognize the power and value of a DIVERSE talent pool and then to FIND Talent, GET Talent, KEEP Talent, GROW Talent and REGENERATE the Talent through the DEI of ACHIEVEMENT™ life cycle process. In doing so, you will create an INCLUSIVE and diverse community/organization that provides an objective non-bias opportunity for EQUITY. I call this 360-degree process of human capital talent reflective of your market reality – TALENTification™.

TALENTification allows You the individual and the organizational enterprise, the ability to go as far and as fast as your dreams can take you!

For individuals and organizations to reach their ultimate success level, it is It is about the inclusion and alignment of everybody to its Values, Vision, Mission, Goals and Purpose and the exclusion of no one.

Using your Diversity as your strategic advantage, is a force multiplier to any individual or organization. However, using Diversity to imply one is better or entitled, solely on their Diversity, is disingenuous ... And doing so in the pursuit of violating ethical, legal or moral conduct is both reprehensible and demeaning to the purpose of Diversity, Equity and Inclusion or one's sense of Belonging.

One's Diversity comes with great responsibility and accountability, not just for oneself, but for what it means to and for others coming alongside and behind. Miss using one's Diversity to project elitism, arrogance and disrespect to oneself, one's position, one's job merely derails the positive that can come from DEI.

"Culture eats strategy for breakfast."

A widely debated phrase attributed to the late Peter Drucker, while it does not appear in any of his 39 books, it will be demonstrated in this book and the result research by several esteemed bodies, to include the INSEAD business school in Paris that reflects only 20% of 450 London-based directors and board members reported investing any significant time or resources to manage and improve it. While the same holds true in research of the Fortune 1,000 global businesses and my research with the Managing Partners of the leading global CPA firms within AICPA!

Tracking most HR and Talent endeavors and initiatives across the past four-decades in my work with 30 of the global Fortune 100 Firms, an array of mid-cap size businesses, entrepreneurial start-ups and with more than 40-Adjutant Generals of State National Guard organizations, are more about maintenance issues and rarely move the needle as a market differential or accelerator to meaningfully quantifiable ROI. And, in most circumstances sadly are mere compliance-oriented institutions and mindsets. If TALENTification is done smartly it is one of the top 2 critical factors in the C-Suite of tomorrow!

Diversity education, awareness, acknowledgement and implementation does not mean nor imply the identification of any one segmentation for inclusion and development, at the detriment of any other one existing segmentation. It is about the inclusion of any one segmentation that can bring value to your organization and that is willing to apply themselves equally among others for meaningful and not token contribution.

Whether you call it **DEI** or any other strategic name, the reality of global smart business is to create an environment that embraces:

D = DIVERSITY = All of the variables that influence us as differences throughout our life … Incorporating ethnicity, race, social-economic background, educational levels, veteran or non-veteran, physical stature and situation, culture, faith-religion and antisemitism, generational, geographical representation and conditioning, life-style (LGBTQ+), experiences, trade and craft, work-groups, handicap and accessibility-needs, etc. – aligned to your organizational values

Diversity for merely the sake of diversity is not diversity, it will always end-up being just another form of discrimination, disingenuousness and only creates future problems.

Think of diversity or community as people as all of the ways people differ …

E = EQUITY = Creating a fair playing field for all people, that may not have had the same starting point as other, to be able to participate if they so make that choice ... From their quantifiable efforts, contributions and net value to the organization and customers served, are equitably honored, compensated, rewarded, awarded, incentivized appropriately, fairly and equitably meritocracy – aligned to your organizational values ...

Think of this as the process and outcomes ...

I = INCLUSION = The sense of "belonging" and appreciation actuality of people of all individuals at any level and within all areas of an organization – aligned to your organizational values ... A true sense of belonging whereby input and participation are created, welcomed, expected and appreciated.

Inclusion is about individuals being able to stand-up, show-up and showcase their amazing talents to serve others, it is about everyone equally being given the opportunity to shut-up, put-up and actually work/participate.

Think of this as people always have a voice ... However, inclusivity does not give license that one must indulge stupidity!

In looking DEI it is always important to see it through the lens of the influencers in your environment, whether that be the laws, culture, safety, relations, etc.

Professor Lionel **Paolella of the University Of Cambridge, Judge Business School Executive Education**, adds beyond the above DEI framework definitions, that any DEI program a business undertakes should strive to produce the highest level of *diversity*, adopt fair and *equitable* treatment for all, and don't neglect to *include* everyone.

DEI is about finding the best talent, creating opportunities for Talent you may be missing or inadvertently overlooking. It is about creating pathways of opportunity for Talent to apply themselves equally and advance ... DEI for the disingenuous is about quotas or attempting to right what they believe are historical inequalities, and that is not what DEI-of-TALENTIFICATION is about.

DEI initiatives, programs and stewards should never use this as a weapon of quotas or an instrument to re-write one's perspective of history.

Whether you frame the conversation and management around diversity or community phrasing, equity or merit of contribution, inclusion or opportunity gateways, DEI is the global reality and so too should it be yours.

If the discussion is to be about Inclusion of Diversity (And, Diversity is not solely a discussion of ethnicity!), then peak performance is a non-negotiable of EVERY Task, Duty, and Responsibility assigned to a job position/role/function to be populated by an individual and if the organization and top tier customers have been made a Brand Promise, then every member of that organization must deliver on that Brand Promise of TDRs – Every time!

If there are gross negative generalizations of any D demographic, than it is dependent upon everyone and especially that generalization D stereotype to demonstrate how absurd, unfair and untrue that generalization is!

When you have an environment that champions the best of your human capital talent and allows for it to always be mindful of your organization and industry's history, addresses current market needs, and recognizes the realities necessary to remain cutting edge and relevant for tomorrow, then you will understand the individuals phases or elements of the DEI of ACHIEVEMENT process of TALENTification.

Organizations that will survive and thrive in the future will be more than agile, creative, cutting edge, and willing to embrace a culture of inclusion and engagement. They will be viewed through the lens of how they manage their people assets – and the number one asset the marketplace has to offer for tomorrow reflects a massive paradigm shift to organizational dynamics from the past 100 plus years – How does one explore the 360-degrees of or the **DEI of TALENTification** is all about **Human Capital!**

For a moment, think back one century in any nation's business history. If you could identify the top 10 major business organizations/employers (non-governmental), what was their business segmentation? Who were their customers? Did they view personnel as human capital or mere labor? Were they inclusive and employ a rich diversity of talent? How did they unleash their human capital for their business life cycle? If we took a look at the United States of America from 1900 moving forward by ten-year increments to today, we would see a long list of giants that no longer exist – not because the business deliverables or distribution systems no longer exist or are no longer needed. In every instance, the industries and exacting businesses that eroded their position, devolved because they did not see their labor talent as human capital; so that human capital left to become the next generation of business entities and leaders.

Everything you need to know and do to survive and thrive is within the human capital of your organization – everything.

Finding great talent used to be like finding the proverbial needle in a haystack. The reality today is that the entire haystack must be seen as talent and the ability to match needs with talent is both an art and a science. The need for organizations to understand the diverse demographics of TALENTification to human capital and all of its' implications within the organization is critical – few understand and even fewer will execute effectively to attain organizational greatness.

While there are countless case studies, books and academic research papers today on the topic of "talent" and a long line of subject-matter experts available, what is missing is a quantifiable data, real-time publication that bridges the academic with the practitioner and is derived from real- world best practices. We see so many new publications across the spectrum addressing topics within talent management as if the topic is new, or there is some new imperative or insight. In actuality, most of the contemporary challenges organizational leaders experience, have been the same ones faced for the past several decades.

What we know today about talent (people) we've known for decades: it's been consistent, yet we keep talking about the same struggles, the same mistakes, the same challenges. We see the same findings coming up today in any number of surveys that we saw 10-20 years ago (e.g., IBM CEO & CHRO surveys; McKinsey, Conference Board, PWC) - why?

Our bias and unconscious bias keeps directing us off trajectory for greater success and when we recognize the answers lie within the diversity of our talent pools and our ability to attract, cultivate, develop, succession and grow future talent through inclusive endeavors, we all win. Bloomberg Asia lead by DEI Global leader Alisha Fernando speaks of their winning culture, "Cultures within cultures, lead to the talent pool you have. When you are inclusive your talent pool will be more diverse and successful.

*It's not about finding the silver bullet, or finding the newest idea about talent, it is about **executing** on what we know. "Executing" the DEI-of-TALENTification is the keystone to actually changing this endless quest.*

This DEI Strategy provides a macro practical approach to the entire concept of "talent" as a life cycle and can be used by any level professional in organizations today.

For decades, I have been an advocate, writing and making the case for human-capital talent-management understanding on a global enterprise basis (C-Suite, Board and Key Stakeholders) within organizations and among thought leaders. It has only been in the past few years that this concept has caught on as a reality among the C-Suite and human-capital constituents within trade organizations like: The Society of Human Resource Managers (SHRM), Association for Talent Development (ATD), the National Speakers Association (NSA), and evolving CEO groups like Vistage, C12, CEOClubs, Young Presidents Organization (YPO), Young Entrepreneurs Organization (YEO), National Association Women Business Owners (NAWBO), and many others.

TALENTification is the 360-degree view of human-capital talent as it applies within an organization and to individuals. TALENTification must be an enterprise-wide endeavor owned by the Chief Learning Officer, or the equivalent, and supported at the C-Suite level. It must also be simple so that implementation becomes assured. When all of the implications of talent management are understood, embraced and actualized by both individuals and organizations, the organization becomes enormously effective, empowered, engaged and envied by others.

To accelerate this level of effectiveness, TALENTification must be aligned with and calibrated from the organization's Values, Vision and Commitments – These are actualized by the organization's key human capital.

TALENTification does not solely mean the engagement of an individual that you are grooming for the C-Suite. It is about growing and developing every individual (not just those being groomed for future senior-level roles), to be the best they can be for themselves and the organization.

Organizations that do this are more effective and have a lower turnover cost. There are many studies that show the high failure rate of bringing in external talent for senior roles... just another reason to develop the talent you already have.

DEI-of-TALENTification also requires specific roles for its' human capital or talent pool:

1. Senior Leaders (Executive Development Programming [EDP] Level) must own the Vision and are the Macro architects of DEI and TALENTification; Their presence should reflect the labor

demographics of the organization and the market they serve; Their participation, representation and advocacy should be felt within any DEI initiative, group, voice;

2. HR Hiring Managers & Talent Management Personnel (Leadership Development Programming [**LDP**] Level and Human Resources) own the roles of Ambassadors, Educators & Accountability Compliance Partners, and data collection specialists of DEI and TALENTification;

3. Supervising Managers (Management Development Programming [**MDP**] Level) serve as the frontline Implementation and serve as the Executors, Developers, Mentors, Sponsors, and Coaches of DEI and TALENTification;

4. Personnel/Employees-at-large (Employee Development Programming [**EDP**]) have the responsibility of being Advocates, Participants, Peer-Mentors, and Influencers at all levels in embracing the ACHIEVEMENT Model process; A ground up voice should be present through an Employee Engagement Group/Employee Resource Group [**EEG/ERG**] that champions among may cultural and quality of work-life issues, DEI;

5. Outsourced Partners must assume the associated roles that they are engaged to fulfill within the ACHIEVEMENT process, whether that is serving in the role of execution, compliance or accountability partners of DEI and TALENTification;

6. Vendor/Service Partners should also be acquainted with the organization's TALENTification ACHIEVEMENT process to assist in their best-practice abilities where applicable of DEI and TALENTification; And ideally their organizations should have a policy and program of DEI and TALENTification;

7. All Knowledge, Skill and Ability **(KSA)** development initiatives and professionals carrying out Organizational Development, Training or Educational endeavors must ensure that what they do, in any format or distribution channel, is in alignment with the TALENTification process and strengthens the ACHIEVE-MENT process of diversity and inclusion, whatever its specific micro role may be, of DEI and TALENTification.

8. For individuals and teams to reach peak performance within your organization, it is essential that clearly defined Tasks, Duties and Responsibilities **(TDR)** and goals be articulated and written out for clarity of all parties and embrace the organizations goals towards of DEI and TALENTification.

Individuals and organizations that are truly vested in each other, experience higher levels of Return on Investment **(ROI)** - return-on-interpersonal relationships, return-on-intellectual capital and return-on-investments. In fact, there is massive research that quantifies that the organizations that embrace DEI and have a diverse workforce, management and leadership teams and diversity among their Boards, demonstrate much higher scores on customer survey and greater profits on their balance sheets.

From innovation and execution, to proactive commitment and higher levels of sense-of-community. From increased Key Performance Indicators **(KPIs)** of achievement, success, and inspired energy to greater levels of drive or ownership to a culture of purpose. With each element in the ownership wheel of effectiveness embracing and feeding off of one another, understanding the Talent life cycle and how it is interrelated, takes a mindset of tomorrow, focused upon today, and reflective of yesterday.

What research has found is when individuals experience success in what they do and when organizations have people aligned doing that which they are best calibrated to do and want to do, then the output is typically one of high quality and quantity and people become committed, almost addicted, to wanting to experience more of that success. TALENTification is the formula to this achieved and sustained reality.

Understanding the life cycle of TALENTification is critical, and after decades of discussion, academic research and volumes of policy wonks advocating various aspects of the topic, the real data still shows a massively flawed approach and multitudes of failures. *Human Resource Executive* shares research from the immediate past 20 years that reflects failures at an alarming rate. Even leading HR/Accounting Consultancy groups like KPMG show internal audits of their own new hires onboarding process as "not very engaging," which leads to 10 percent to 25 percent of new hires leaving their organization; this same ratio was reflected with their Clients. The associated direct and indirect costs to these percentages are staggering.

Korn Ferry Futurestep division takes the issue of DEI TALENTification from the onboarding and integration phases in our model and have found that the statistics are even more alarming. An industry survey of their clients and marketplace found that as many as 98 percent indicated onboarding programs are key to recruitment and retention, with 69 percent indicating they have formal onboarding programs on paper to touch all employees. Yet, only 23 percent have legitimate engaged programs that last one day, and 30 percent indicate theirs last only one week, with no KPIs beyond those dates.

My own work with CEO-to-CEO Peer groups like: *VISTAGE, C12, CEOClubs, YPO globally, YEO, NAWBO,* and National Guard General Officers nationally, reinforces these trends and critical points that have led to the ACHIEVEMENT model.

Look at TALENTification as a 360-degree initiative or endeavor. There are eleven interlinked phases, I have identified as the ACHIEVEMENT process model. Each one blending to and from one another and every level providing real-time feedback that can be plugged in at any other stage for clarification and enhanced ROI.

There are countless human resourcing and psychological diagnostic instruments, online portals, and professional service firms available, which can all be deployed within each of the following talent metrics for more in-depth analytics and data-collection benchmarking for an organization, executive team development and guidance, business owner or human resources professional's considerations.

The ***ACHIEVEMENT*™** *of **DEI**-of-**TALENTification*™ consists of understanding and thoroughly executing the entire life cycle process:

ACHIEVEMENT Model

1. **A** – **A**wareness of DEI TALENT life cycle

2. **C** – **C**larify DEI Identification of Needs

3. **H** – **H**uman-Capital Acquisition & DEI

4. **I** – **I**ntegrate DEI & On-Boarding Talent

5. **E** – **E**ngage, Activate & Socialization of DEI

6. **V** – **V**est all in the DEI Process

7. **E** – **E**nhance thru DEI Development & Management

8. **M** – **M**ove DEI Talent thru Succession

9. **E** – **E**valuate your DEI Model or Process

10. **N** – **N**ext Steps and Post Mortem Analysis of DEI

11. **T** – **T**each the Organization DEI-of-*TALENTification*

One final point:

We know from numerous studies spanning several decades that turnover is very expensive and it is much less costly to keep your talent, especially great talent, than to replace it. I believe DEI-of-TALENTification will help organizations reduce their turnover and significantly increase their market dominance.

Here is a fast-track overview of the talent life cycle dashboard process:

1. **Awareness of DEI TALENT Life Cycle** – The talent vision must be articulated by the C-Suite and owned by that population demographic, if the organization is ever to believe and buy into the value of any DEI program and goals.

   The best way to look at human capital talent, is through the 5Ws & 1H model. The Why, Who, What, When, Where, and How. In order to achieve this one must be as diverse in this approach and outreach as possible for the market space one is in. A clear non bias understanding to the terms of Diversity, Equity and Inclusion must be undertaken. To address our talent pool needs for today and tomorrow can only occur when one is willing to explore talent from:

   Human Capital Talent Outlook Report - All of the variables that influence us as differences throughout our life … Incorporating ethnicity, race, social-economic background, educational levels, veteran or non-veteran, physical stature and situation, culture, faith-religion and antisemitism, generational, geographical representation and conditioning, life-style (LGBTQ+), experiences, trade and craft, work-groups, handicap and accessibility-needs, etc. – aligned to your organizational values. Create three data spreadsheets to start your process:

#1 … what your organization looks like today; % of demographic breakout,

#2 … what your customer base looks like today; % of demographic breakout,

#3 … what the geography that you can pull from and operate within looks like today; % of demographic breakout,

Fascinatingly, the data that spreadsheet #2 and #3 show, will provide you with data to evaluate what #1 looks like today. You can see how diversity appears in your organization today and what your goals may need to become to remain relevant in the future.

Equity and Inclusion will reveal itself in your spreadsheet #1 and then you can evaluate #1 further as you look at the pyramid of labor within your organization, from the bottom frontline to the top C-Suite. What does diversity look like throughout your organization and where are there opportunities for diversity enhancement, opportunities for equity of growth and participation and levels of inclusion missed.

Your DEI Strategy should come from this data observation, the underserved demographics within your own organization, and what your talent pool reality must reflect for the future.

Why do I need this talent (in conjunction with the business strategy); Who is this talent; What do they need to do; When do I need them; Where will they be in the organization; and, How will I get them. The talent-management life cycle concept includes: the Planning and Forecasting of Human-Capital Needs against Positions, Organizational, Market, Growth, P&L, and Attrition Management needs; How does this integrate into Business Plans, Mission Statements, Values and Brand Promise; Design career and positional pathways for organizational alignment and effectiveness Talent Life Cycle (cradle to grave): *Clarify your needs ICW the Business strategy ⌧ Acquire ⌧ Integrate ⌧ Engage ⌧ Develop ⌧ Move ⌧ Evaluate people and process ⌧ Repeat*

Understanding DEI as not a quota or race initiative, but substantially more in alignment to good business is critical to individual and leadership thinking. There are three human resource paradigms of the past decades that influence how many in your organization will view TALENTification and DEI – The ASSIMILIATION paradox of new talent should assimilate to me/us will be a dealbreaker to you, The DIFFERENTIATION paradox is about exclusion and others are not like me/us and therefore we don't want them, will also be a dealbreaker to you, The INTEGRATION paradox is the new model about inclusion and how we can leverage the best of one another so we all win!

Four core elements to be considered and executed in the implementation of your DEI-of-TALENTification process:

One – Implementing and Communicating the Organizations DEI Talent Strategy – **Determine your DEI Strategy**

Second – Establish the governance structure – **Choice of WHAT this will be for you and HOW it is to be executed**

Third – Identify the key metrics to be used and measured for progress/goals – **Clarify that everyone understands**

Fourth – Empower diversity leaders, champions and advocates to engage everyone – **Commitment of whether your people willing & Congruence to your Culture and Values**

"Top-down support is crucial, and bottom up involvement is critical" to any inclusive DEI talent program, it must be holistic to work, as Professor Lionel **Paolella of the University Of Cambridge, Judge Business School Executive Education** has found through his research.

2. **Clarify DEI Identification of Needs** – With the "Awareness" in hand via DEI talent audits, what do you expect the new talent to do, i.e., what are the Tasks you expect them to perform, what Duties will they have, and what Responsibilities will they have **(TDR)**. This must be done first because it leads into the next crucial step: what KSAs are required to perform the role (TDR) you plan to put them in. There is nothing new here regarding TDR and KSA. What is new, is our focus on executing these two things to perfection. You must be deliberate, objective, and relentless in doing both of these thoroughly, as everything for successful Talentification follows from this. Having the right roles, with the correct TDRs tied to the business strategy, leads you to finding the right people with the right KSA. Also, this must be done with a short-term/long-term view. You are clearly trying to satisfy immediate, near-term requirements, but you must also be cognizant of the future so the talent you bring in can grow with the organization over time.

Recognize that diversity is not just about female versus male or black versus white, it is more importantly about the experiences, abilities, insights and wisdom that a diverse talent pool brings in addressing needs and seeing potential derailments and opportunities within the organization.

Key Performance Indicators **(KPIs)**: *Analytics of Positional Needs and the corresponding competencies associated with each trait/task deliverable needed for effective execution of Positional Needs; Constituents' Buy-In levels; Task v. Traits Analysis Needs, Core Skill Requirements v. Acceptable; What is a Subject-Matter Expert by function/position/strategic levels; Planning; Forecasting of Human-Capital Needs against Positions, Organizational, Market, Growth, P&L, and Attrition Management needs; Utilizing the Player Capability Indexing Model™ to objectively assess talent; SWOT Timelines of Now v. Future; Talent life cycle by Position, Tenure, Individual Aspirations, Organizational Needs, Market Needs and Attrition Needs; Identification of applicable social-style, personality-style and capacity-style assessment instruments and how those analytics reveal compatibility of individuals with the organization, specific teams and overall brand; Etc.*

3. **Human-Capital Acquisition & DEI** – You are now ready to identify where the talent you need is and how to go about recruiting them (internally or externally). Acquiring talent should be a simple multi-phased process. You may need to consider the systems you use and the people interactions for finding, interviewing and hiring diverse talent, as sometimes unconscious bias may cause you to miss the best talent in the market place. You may need to consider if your processes intimidate perspective candidates from even applying, and if so develop solutions, include individuals of diversity from within your organization

now to provide advise on how to improve your outreach approach and interviewing practices.

Too often we see organizations designing very robust, but convoluted processes, using numerous external search agencies for the same job or talent pool. Simple processes are easy to implement, easy to explain to the organization and hiring manager, and result in quicker placements. A simple but thorough job specification/description is the first step (generated through a coordinated effort of the hiring manager with the human resources manager). Advertising and sourcing should be done through the organization's website, targeted external social media networking portals, and select search firms, i.e. those that have expertise in the domain you are recruiting for. If your organization seems to out-of-balance from a diversity perspective, consider applications that hide contact name and geographical references, so you can focus on actual work experience and abilities to find and vet better candidates.

Consider a more global and through outreach for example if you are wanting college graduates, are you establishing communication connections with 100 percent of the institutions in your geography? And, with key contacts and advocates win each of those institutions. Are you possibly creating an Employee Resource Group (ERG) of a diverse cross section of your talent pool and involving them in this first critical step? Recognize from your Human Capital Talent Outlook Report (spreadsheet), that you may need to connect into different venues, locations and individuals to find diversity talent, if it is not within your present networks and outreach initiatives.

Consider both **Clarification & Identification of Needs** and **Human-Capital Acquisition** as having to ebb-and-flow back-and-forth with one another to be fluid and effective for your DEI goals … For example to ensure that Implicit Bias nor Unconscious Bias influence these two critical elements of the ACHIEVEMENT Model, ensure that what you post, how you post, where you post the openings does not drive talent away before you ever meet.

KPIs: *Designing instruments and pathways for Attracting those Needs (organic, service bureaus, agents, online portals, etc.); Use skill based assessments; Remove language or requirements that may suggest a bias; Use software to facilitate blind interviews; Promotion and Marketing of Needs; Interviewing and Vetting Process/Systems/Instruments to Gain the Appropriate and Best Human Capital Available; Addressing Biases; Ensuring Aspirations of Candidate Prospects match Organization and internal Key Constituents.*

4. **Integrating DEI & Onboarding Talent** – Getting new hires to the organization in a quick, efficient and robust way has shown to be one of the biggest factors in attitude formation by these new hires. This is much more than pointing people to a vast amount of information posted on the organization's website; it is essential that there is a personal, human touch to onboarding and integrating people into the organization and into their new role. The speed with which people become knowledgeable and effective in their role is accelerated by the assimilation. The popularity of books like "The First 90 Days" or "Right From The Start" are a testament to this.

Onboarding talent should also be a reflection of the DEI goals of the organization. Here is where you may want to pause and reflect on the uniqueness of the individual and tailor that onboarding experience for the first 30-60-90-120-days from both an HR process needs and the supervising manager area as well. Provide a DEI-Sponsor or Advocate to serve as a secondary talent resource to ensure the new hire feels a sense of belonging, inclusion and is valued.

All next steps aligned with previous KPIs: *30-, 60-, 90-, 120-day minimum formal structured integration and check-up checkpoints; Technician v. Operational Effectiveness milestones; Ensuring new Talent blend, support and grow Business Plans, Mission Statements and Values; Talent life cycle process identified and initiated by Position, Tenure, Individual Aspirations, Organizational Needs, Compliance to Job Position Statements, Market Needs and Attrition Needs; Initial Professional Development Plans* **(PDP)** *and needs aligned with individual aspirations; Assigned a sponsor or mentor as secondary alignment resource; Artificial Intelligence* **(AI)** *is a player; Champions; Etc.*

5. **Engage, Activate & Socialization of DEI** – All next steps aligned with previous KPIs: *Acceptance, Participation, Comfort, Sense of Belonging; Introducing and Advocating & Sponsoring New Talent into Organization and to Core Personalities; Talent life cycle by Position, Tenure, Individual Aspirations, Organizational Needs, Market Needs and Attrition Needs; Transfer of Learning & Creating the Learning Mindset Virally; Mentoring; Standard-of-Conduct Policies; Engaging the TALENTification Terrorist; Etc.*

Here is where talent decides to stay and contribute (engaged, inclusive), stay and go through the motions (complacent) or leave. Along with great managerial-leadership engagement and on-going coaching, you may want to explore other strategies, processes and programs that creates inclusion and provides pathways for equity in performance and opportunities. Create an Employee Resource Group (ERG), Employee Engagement Group (EEG) or Diversity Engagement Groups (DEG), to serve as talent advocates and diversity champions. Have a performance review check-ins or electronic assessments to gather on-going feedback.

Explore, develop and implement employee driven peer-to-peer recognition and achievement programs to further serve organically bottom-up behaviors you seek, along with top-down managerial-leadership same programs.

Create DEI specific assessments for feedback by all employees and not just new hires in the onboarding processes or in-boarding of internal talent that moves or is promoted with, that seeks just feedback on Diversity, Equity and Inclusion factors you want to track or need to track.

Career pathways and journey experiences should be considered for all employees here and especially as you reflect on the Diversity spreadsheet exercise in the ACHIEVEMENT Model **Awareness of DEI TALENT Life Cycle** step and the Human Capital Talent Outlook Report. Consider programs like Emerging Talent, Next-Gen, Emerging Leaders, or affinity development tracks like 20-under-20 or 30-under-30 talent programs or Emerging Women in Business/Leadership or Diversity

Accelerators (there is no good way to name some of these initiatives) … The objective is to provide an accelerated development pathway for previously underrepresented groups that your organization can benefit from including.

6. **Vest all in the DEI Process** – Often in the talent arena, Human Resources either assumes total responsibility or managers defer their responsibility to Human Resources. The most effective organizations have a holistic approach to TALENTization, where many people have equal responsibility to identify and clarify needs, find and acquire the right people, assimilate them into the organization quickly and help them succeed while they are there. Having operational managers and the human resources department equal owners of the organization's talent is essential, and having senior executives engaged and involved with all processes ensures that only the essential activities are focused on. If there was a "silver bullet" for TALENTization, it is that the organization's most important and valuable asset is its people, and that the organization's executives, operational managers, and human resources are all focused on maximizing this asset.

Inclusion is the objective here. The more you can provide individuals with meaningful opportunities to share, learn, grow and serve, the organization will always be the beneficiary. Again, here is where you can task, grow and challenge individuals, business groups, the ERG can be a major champion in the DEI Organizational goal attainment, from both a grassroots level and as proactive players in organizational policy implementation. Provide opportunities for feedback of how people feel DEI is being actualized and always create a climate and culture of solutions whenever problems may be identified. Work hard here to ensure levels of bias (Unconscious, Categorization and Affinity) do not create barriers to success, and identify early and fast any barriers that arise, so they can be addressed.

Consider Employee Resource Groups (ERG), Employee Engagement Groups (EEG) or Diversity Network Groups for individual affinity if appropriate, like: Women's Staff, LGBTQ+, Race Equality, Disabled, Veterans, Parents, Alumni, Customer feedback, Governance, Leadership, Cross-team, etc.

Explore, develop and implement employee driven peer-to-peer recognition and achievement programs to further serve organically bottom-up behaviors you seek, along with top-down managerial-leadership same programs.

Identify ways to include everyone in activities, socialization, work projects and celebrations, to gain a better respect and appreciation for the diversity among us and the rewards for us.

All next steps aligned with previous KPIs: *Gaining Ownership, Buy-In, Empowerment, Free-Will Engagement, Proactive Mindset & Behaviors; Continuous human-capital growth and challenges; Talent life cycle by Position, Tenure, Individual Aspirations, Organizational Needs, Market Needs and Attrition Needs; Mentoring/Champions; Etc.*

7. **Enhance Through DEI Development & Management** – With great talent acquired, integrated and onboarded, assimilated into their role and team so they are engaged, the next focus area is to manage their performance so they can excel and to develop them throughout their career with the organization. Effective performance management is critical for excellence and for

creating a bench of leaders to allow the organization to continue to grow and replace senior leaders over time. Development of talent has a dual purpose: One is to continue to advance skills for a person's current role and the other is to prepare them for future roles, whether lateral or a promotion, or whether in the same region or global.

To grow your DEI talent, consider creating job experiences that have stretch assignment, opportunities to work cross diversity lines and inclusion with talent that some would otherwise never cross paths with. Mento both new talent, peer-to-peer talent and establish reverse Mentor opportunities for younger or diverse talent to engage the established talent within an organization. Consider how often you provide structured formal and informal performance reviews? Within these opportunities consider creating additional assessment questions to gather feedback on individuals perspective on DEI initiatives, processes, programs and opportunities from their user experience.

All next steps aligned with previous KPIs: *Pipeline flow of Human Capital on a daily/weekly/monthly basis; Deployment of six core Managerial, Leadership, Coaching, Motivation Interventions (via the Managerial-Leadership-Coaching L-Grid™); Managing Career Pathing; Effective and timely developmental Performance Assessments or Reviews for growth optics; Facilitation of regular legitimate meaningful Professional Development Plans and, as/when appropriate, Professional Improvement Plans; Discussions tied to Career-Pathing; AI is a player; TALENT Horizon Report - Succession Development Span-of-Influence Chart; Etc.*

8. **Move DEI Talent Through Succession** – A succession plan is essential to insure the organization is thinking about the future. Ideally you want to have a succession plan for every supervisor role and higher, but from an organizational leadership perspective it's essential to identify the roles critical to the organization's success and to have a robust succession process for those roles. Ask yourself as you make these evaluations, what does the diversity and inclusion look like as you track from employee up through to the senior positions in your organization. Are we growing a diverse inclusion talent pool today and for tomorrow. As we move talent through our organizational journey map, does it reflect that we are as diverse as we need to be to be relevant? Are we as inclusive at every level as we should be? Are people of all diversity being equitably treated throughout the organization? Is this an organization that our people are advocates in their own sphere-of-influence when they are not at work?

In fact, part of an organization's fiduciary responsibility, and part of the Board of Directors' responsibility, is to review the succession plan annually. A key part of succession is linking it to the business strategy. The business strategy is future looking, and succession should be as well – where is the organization going and what kinds of talent will be needed to make sure the strategy succeeds? Succession runs hand-in-hand with development; by identifying internal talent for critical future roles you can focus development so the right person is ready for the right job at the right time.

Are we benchmarking our developmental plans against what individual employee's expectations are? How do we measure against others best-in-class in our industry and geography today?

Be aware of Micro Aggressions (verbal, environmental, behaviors, policies, actions, etc.) that can cause one to feel unwelcomed, not included, valued and underappreciated, work to eliminate and educate others to these as barriers to success.

KPIs: *Exploring how to promote and who is promotable from your five levels of Stars & Performers; Benchmark against your TALENT Horizon Report-Succession Development Span-of-Influence Chart; Etc.;*

9. **Evaluate Your DEI Model or Process** – DEI should be about open pathways for everyone and then 100 percent true merit based upon quantifiable data, not personal opinions, from the frontline to the executive room. This is the data analysis phase, and built off of the data collected at each previous level in the ACHIEVEMENT Model. Along with any established data collection KPIs you track, also consider data around: Trends in business, Risk Management items, Customer needs and satisfaction, Customer experiences with you, Supply chain, Compliance, DEI, People performance, etc. Create transparent dashboards of data that you want people to see, to drive DEI goals into actuality.

All next steps aligned with previous KPIs: *Planning; Forecasting of Human-Capital Needs against Positions, Creating of WPxF=ROI formulas, Organizational, Market, Growth, P&L, Individual Needs/Aspirations/Goals; Attrition Management needs, etc.; How does this integrate into Business Plans, Mission Statements and Values; Benchmark against your talent audits by individual, business unit needs and organizational strategic planning,*

3-Deep Mindset; Radical Relevance/RE5 Modeling applied here; Etc.

10. **Next Steps and Post Mortem Analysis of DEI(A)** – On a regular cycle (Quarterly or Annually) pull together a cross population of DEI key stakeholders (key employees, ERG leaders, HR team, core business unit leaders and the C-Suite) to discuss where your goals were at the beginning of the year and where are we now? Evaluate how people are participating (voluntarily stepping up and in, is it cross team involvement and participation, are we setting and achieving goals, who is included in the goals and making strides, who is just along for the rind, and who are the outliers) …?

How are we including and celebrating successes along the way? How are we encouraging socialization.

Review the DEI Strategy and evaluate any adjustments necessary, consider the four core elements to be considered and executed in the DEI-of-TALENTification process discussed at the beginning of the ACHIEVEMENT model and how well are you executing on:

One – Implementing and Communicating the Organizations DEI Talent Strategy

Second – Establish the governance structure

Third – Identify the key metrics to be used and measured for progress/goals

Fourth – Empower diversity leaders, champions and advocates to engage everyone

Remember, "Top-down support is crucial, and bottom-up involvement is critical" to any inclusive DEI talent program, it must be holistic to work, as Professor Lionel **Paolella of the University Of Cambridge, Judge Business School Executive Education** has found through his research, so what does your data reveal about how you are executing.

Create a macro guide or check list of inclusive best-practices that everyone at every level with the organizations can benchmark their own behaviors, actions, comments and commitments against to ensure the culture and organization you have, seek or desire to maintain is always strengthened by every action and initiative and that no one consciously (bias) or unconsciously (bias) allows for great talent to be pushed aside and be made to feel unwelcomed. You can get insights from several global trade associations such as:

- www.shrm.org - SHRM - The Voice of All Things Work
- www.td.org – ATD | The World's Largest Talent Development Association | ATD

All next steps aligned with previous KPIs: *Exit Interviews, Benchmarking, and SWOT Analysis against every human-capital need on an individual and organizational level; How does this integrate into Business Plans, Mission Statements and Values; Ensuring Inclusion and Diversity equal to marketplace; Onboarding the Retired Superstars; Etc.*

11. **Teach the Organization DEI-of-TALENTification: Relaunch/Evolution** – DEI-of-TALENTification is not a one time program or event, it is a continuous journey. All next steps

aligned with previous KPIs: *Best Practice Management, Lessons Learned Implementations; Benchmark against industry or trade association analytics; recalibration as appropriate; The C-Suite consideration; Etc.*

The need for organizations to understand, from cradle to grave, the TALENTification **ACHIEVEMENT**™ model and how it impacts the number one asset, that of your human capital talent is critical.

If we do TALENTification right, yes, we may from time-to-time find and develop and nurture and grow phenomenal talent, that will leave us ... And that is a great experience to know you have participated in the creation of phenomenal talent that will go and benefit others. And, if we do this correctly, that person will model you and further develop phenomenal talent for others.

Keep in mind, like-begets-like and disingenuous bad actors can manipulate and hide behind DEI and create a bad taste in others minds – stand up against this!

The DEI of human capital and all of its' implications within the organization is critical – few understand and even fewer will execute effectively to attain market greatness. Often, we find different constituents within an organization own a few of each of these areas; yet, no one typically understands and manages the entire process. And that is why talent management within most organizations runs internally into conflict and is often ineffective.

The overall employee experience is shaped and determined by how you (individually and organizationally) manage your side of each of the ACHIEVEMENT life cycle phases and what the individual employee receives, sees, observes, and internalizes as their

EXPERIENCE along the way. Every touchpoint from the organization, whether intentional or unintentional, whether overt or not, still shapes the experience an individual has within the work environment. It is clichéd, but always recognize that one bad apple (peer or supervisor) can ruin an organization; It takes massive work to make greatness, and yet, it can be imploded in one simple person.

Talent should just be talent, void of any other defining characteristics. The reality is that we all see through our own glasses, biased or not, conscious or not. Looking at all of the talent available through the lens of DEI merely holds one accountable to recognizing we all do not look alike.

And, no matter who you are, you are the "D" in Diversity, it is not "D" for them or "D" for me, it is "D" for all of us!

Consider TALENT in a multiple of applications, and for an organization it demands the understanding of each application and how they must align as one for ultimate ROI. Identify at each of the following five TALENT considerations: what do you expect the new talent to do, i.e., what are the TDRs. This must be done first because it leads into the next crucial step: what KSAs are required to perform the role (TDR) you plan to put them in:

1. TALENT management of the INDIVIDUAL and DEI implications of all;

2. TALENT management of career PATHWAYS and DEI implications of all;

3. TALENT management of critical essential POSITION pathways and DEI implications of all;

4. TALENT management of secondary support POSITION pathways and DEI implications of all;

5. TALENT management of the ORGANIZATION and DEI implications of all.

Understanding the DEI life cycle of TALENTification is critical and we hope this book helps synthesize what we know about human capital and provides a simplified approach for individuals and organizations to move beyond the carousel of the past.

Chapter One

Awareness Of DEI(A) TALENT Life Cycle

Awareness of DEI TALENT Life Cycle – The talent vision must be articulated by the C-Suite and owned by that population demographic, if the organization is ever to believe and buy into the value of any DEI program and goals.

The best way to look at human capital talent, is through the 5Ws & 1H model. The Why, Who, What, When, Where, and How. In order to achieve this one must be as diverse in this approach and outreach as possible for the market space one is in. A clear non bias understanding to the terms of Diversity, Equity and Inclusion must be undertaken. To address our talent pool needs for today and tomorrow can only occur when one is willing to explore talent from:

DEI initiatives, programs and stewards should never use this as a weapon of quotas or an instrument to re-write one's perspective of history, it is about creating a strong viable future.

Whether you frame the conversation and management around diversity or community phrasing, equity or merit of contribution, inclusion or opportunity gateways, DEI is the global reality and so too should it be yours.

Human Capital Talent Outlook Report - Diversity of Demographics, Gender, Ethnicity, Generational, LGBTQ+, Social-Economic Class, Disability, Veteran, Educational-Level, Religion and any other Key Performance Factor you need to and should be aware of to be more effective in the market space of tomorrow. Create three data spreadsheets to start your process:

#1 of what your organization looks like today,

#2 what your customer base looks like today,

#3 what the geography that you can pull from and operate within looks like today.

Fascinatingly, the data that spreadsheet #2 and #3 show, will provide you with data to evaluate what #1 looks like today. You can see how diversity appears in your organization today and what your goals may need to become to remain relevant in the future.

Equity and Inclusion will reveal itself in your spreadsheet #1 and then you can evaluate #1 further as you look at the pyramid of labor within your organization, from the bottom frontline to the top C-Suite. What does diversity look like throughout your organization and where are there opportunities for diversity enhancement, opportunities for equity of growth and participation and levels of inclusion missed.

I'm reminded of a research model from Australian Andrea Wessendorf and the concept of **Intersectionality-of-Diversity**, whereby we can see how we may be advertently working against ourselves and have blind spots around diversity. It can be this *Intersectionality-of-Diversity* that is depriving our organizations from greatness and depriving individuals from greatness. She sues a business for not being hired. The judge rules against her, seeing that the business is hiring "black" men and is hiring white "women". What the judge failed to recognize, was the intersectionality of those two demographics were "black women" that were actually not being hired.

Your DEI Strategy should come from data and observation, the underserved demographics within your own organization, and what your talent pool reality must reflect for the future.

Why do I need this talent (in conjunction with the business strategy); Who is this talent; What do they need to do; When do I need them; Where will they be in the organization; and, How will I get them. The talent-management life cycle concept includes: the Planning and Forecasting of Human-Capital Needs against Positions, Organizational, Market, Growth, P&L, and Attrition Management needs; How does this integrate into Business Plans, Mission Statements, Values and Brand Promise; Design career and positional pathways for organizational alignment and effectiveness Talent Life Cycle (cradle to grave): *Clarify your needs ICW the Business strategy * Acquire * Integrate * Engage * Develop * Move * Evaluate people and process * Repeat*

Understanding DEI as not a quota or race initiative, but substantially more in alignment to good business is critical to individual and leadership thinking. There are three human resource paradigms of the past decades that influence how many in your organization will view TALENTification and DEI – The ASSIMILIATION paradox of new talent should assimilate to me/us will be a dealbreaker to you, The DIFFERENTIATION paradox is about exclusion and others are not like me/us and therefore we don't want them, will also be a dealbreaker to you, The INTEGRATION paradox is the new model about inclusion and how we can leverage the best of one another so we all win!

<u>Four core elements to be considered and executed in the implementation of your DEI-of-TALENTification process</u>:

One – Implementing and Communicating the Organizations DEI Talent Strategy – **Determine your DEI Strategy**

Second – Establish the governance structure – **Choice of WHAT this will be for you and HOW it is to be executed**

Third – Identify the key metrics to be used and measured for progress/goals – **Clarify that everyone understands**

Fourth – Empower diversity leaders, champions and advocates to engage everyone – **Commitment of whether your people willing & Congruence to your Culture and Values**

"Top-down support is crucial, and bottom-up involvement is critical" to any inclusive DEI talent program, it must be holistic to work, as Professor Lionel **Paolella of the University Of Cambridge,**

Judge Business School Executive Education has found through his research.

Again, the best way to look at Human Capital or Talent is the 5Ws & 1H: Why, Who, What, When, Where, and How. Why do I need this talent (in conjunction with the business strategy); Who is this talent; What do they need to do; When do I need them; Where will they be in the organization; and How will I get them. The talent-management life cycle concept includes: Planning; Forecasting of Human-Capital Needs against Positions, Organizational, Market, Growth, P&L, and Attrition Management needs; and importantly, How does this integrate into Business Plans, Mission Statements and Values.

Talent life cycle (cradle to grave): Clarify your needs ICW the Business strategy ⊠ Acquire ⊠ Integrate ⊠ Engage ⊠ Develop ⊠ Move ⊠ Evaluate people and process ⊠ Repeat

What is Human-Capital Talent comprised of; Understanding the Talent-management life cycle concept; Planning; Forecasting of Human-Capital needs against positions, with a view toward Organizational, Market, Growth, P&L, and Attrition Management needs; How does this integrate into Business Plans, Mission Statements, Values and Brand Promise, etc.; What are succession realities; Understanding Positional Pathways, Career Pathways and Individual aspiration pathways.

*

"Everyone wants to be on a championship team;
no one wants to do the practice!"

A great line Basketball Coach Bobby Knight shared with me in an interview piece in www.ProfessionalPerformanceMagazine.com

All organizational success that can be replicated repeatedly is contingent upon five core variables. These same variables must be present throughout every aspect of the ACHIEVEMENT talent process. The first three are bantered so often in organizational leadership that they may seem hollow; however, they are essential. And yet, so many individuals and organizations live by the first three and merely stagger along the survival line daily, never to experience what thriving looks like. Why? It is simple: the last two variables of the five are the difference between surviving and thriving but the last two are also very unpopular within society, organizations and individuals today.

I have found - through my decades of research and active participation with leaders and organizations from private sector to non-profit and from government agencies to military operations - that these five variables are ALWAYS present when success appears and when talent management and development are present. And the last two are always bastardized away when failure and incompetence raises their heads and great talent are run away.

Consider:

1. Strategy/Systems owned by senior leaders and influenced by core values and vision (Owned by the EDP Level)
2. Operations/Process (Owned by the LDP Level)
3. Tactics/ Procedures (Owned by the MDP Level)
4. Execution/Talent (Owned by the Staff Level)

5. Accountability/Human Capital (Owned by all levels)

6. Actions and Activities that are elementary to sustained success, must be identified and articulated to all and is owned by everyone.

So, keeping these five critical factors in play as we work through the eleven elements to execution and ACHIEVEMENT of the talent-management model for a healthy, sustained and engaged organization is your starting point for every consideration and question that may arise.

What is Human-Capital Talent comprised of: 5W & 1H. Looking at the necessity and importance to identifying talent within an organization at every level and how best to attract, develop and retain talent is essential to organizational health and market competitiveness. At the beginning of the talent life cycle, it is important that an organization have a process by which everyone (WHO) has a cursory understanding of WHAT talent management means; HOW all are impacted by it; WHERE the touchpoints are along the talent life cycle; WHEN these touchpoints take place; and WHERE an effective talent life cycle takes place. And at the endpoint, WHY this conversation and activities are even important. The buy-in and ownership by all influencers, stakeholders and leaders will make this a part of a thriving culture of excellence or serve as mere lip service. Everyone at every level plays a role and the awareness of TALENT and the life cycle of the individual, behaviors, output, and roles are all important for both the immediate needs of an organization and the evolving needs of being relevant today and competitive tomorrow.

Understanding the Talent-Management life cycle concept. A path to greatness for everyone within an organization, whether an individual as a contributor wants to remain in their present capacity; an organization needs progression for those onboarded; or when an individual/organization wants to move talent horizontally or vertically within an organization or industry. To efficiently understand an organization and how business practices flow, it is essential in most organizations that there are natural entry-point positions that progress sequentially from one place to another. This understanding and proficiency of how an organization finds great talent, onboards talent, develops and retains talent is a part of the understanding of the life cycle. And how individuals and organizations address talent when it no longer serves a viable role within an organization, is essential.

Planning, Forecasting of Human-Capital needs against positions, Organizational, Market, Growth, P&L, and Attrition Management needs. This is where the science and art of talent life cycle really becomes sophisticated, in how specialized systems and people must become to be effective in serving the organization, key operating positions, businesses and the executive team and boards of an organization. Individuals and peers must all own the task of ensuring that the right talent is grown, developed, supported and held accountable in a non-threatening manner within an organization. If it isn't, the cascading negative ramifications within a business operating area and organization overall will become that organization's cancer and it will spread passive-aggressively if unchecked – every time.

The talent life cycle also needs to address, at every level, the ongoing development of individuals and the why behind it. From onboarding and general individual engagement programming, whether live onsite, online experiential learning platforms, peer-to-peer, coaching, etc., growing an engaged talent force starts at the top with EDP, LDP, and MDP to Staff Development Programming (**SDP**). This developmental programming needs to address both individual developmental pathways and organizational pathway needs, and must be owned by individuals, their leaders and the organization. Many industries have been built around this for so long it has become institutionalized as a pathway to success; how about your organization?

Major accounting firms for decades have made it a talent-acquisition process to hire college accounting and finance grads into their firms for what is really a two-year contract. Within that time frame it gives the organization an opportunity to vet that talent and determine its best pathway within the organization, or not, and all of its talent life cycle mechanisms are impacted accordingly. You show talent performance, you are retained and developed accordingly into a firm practice area and trajectory; or a client may see your talent and hire you away within that two-year time frame; or maybe the talent will transition away from that initial firm or industry. This approach works so effectively, it allows everyone within a firm to recognize if the new employee has talent they can benefit from or not.

This also allows talent the opportunity in reverse to vet the organization, industry, practice area specialization, and determine if it is what they want to commit to as a long-term talent trajectory.

How this integrates to Business Plans, Mission Statements and Values. Here is the birthplace of the talent life cycle. The core values an organization and its leaders have, believe in and demonstrate will drive directly how talent life cycles are really designed and followed. If values are superficial or mere wall placards, you will see an unhealthy talent life cycle, whereby it is survival of the fittest at the end of the day. It is the deep-rooted values that one possesses that generate the visions held by an organization's key leaders that give focus and clarity to the talent within an organization and project outward to talent that may be attracted to an organization. It is from values that we get visions, and that drives the public pronouncements via mission statements that serve as the operational GPS, in essence.

This serves as the framework for how key talent then designs their operating business plans, which serve as road maps to their work flow on a daily, weekly, monthly, quarterly and annual basis. These plans will reveal what talent you have, what talent you need to execute success and will reveal the KPIs along the way. This last document will reveal a lot about talent at the operating level, how one meets immediate needs and how to sustain it. This drives subsequent analytics on the depth of the present talent pool one has, needs, and where the gaps are and will be. As business leaders and individuals, understanding where one lands within a business plan also reveals the ongoing developmental plans, ownership and accountability matrices, as well as the ongoing coaching and performance dashboards.

Benchmarked against succession realities; Understanding Career Pathways and Individual aspiration pathway. Again, from a macro perspective, the awareness of the talent life cycle at the outset is not about getting too detailed as to overwhelm or turn anyone off, it is to raise situational or organizational awareness of how everyone owns a piece and has a stake in effective, engaged understanding of the talent within themselves and the organization, and having the right people, at the right time, involved in the right roles. Truly understanding the reality of the life cycle of positions within an organization and the life cycle of individuals will have a direct impact on talent management. Allowing for these realities is critical for a sustainably healthy organization.

The power, here, is for the organization to have an understanding of what talent looks like in each core role of an organization in order for that role to survive and thrive. It is important for there to be clear pathways from one position to another and from one level within a work area or organization to the next, so everyone knows the progression pathway and the why and how of that pathway – whether that flow is horizontal or vertical within an organization. Building institutional and industry talent development is a process with a clear architecture and some critical developmental stepping stones along the way, and the talent life cycle is critical to the health and wealth of any enterprise.

As you start into this talent process, let your values be your GPS at every step and with each decision. When values are in conflict at any level or with any key stakeholder, then you have established a crack in your talent system that will be the source of pain points throughout the process and among individuals.

Think of the chain metaphor – A chain is only as strong as its weakest link. Talent is a link and the chain, is the Talent life cycle. Understanding what each link is there for; what each link must be comprised of; and how each link interconnects to one another to accomplish what purpose, is the AWARENESS phase of the eleven-stage TALENTification process.

Pull together ideas from your previous work experiences, whereby human capital was at the forefront of decisions. Examine the organizations that you have been involved with that understood that everyone had a stake in looking out for new talent to be onboarded. Wherein everyone understood that best talent within an organization, at every level, made for a more effective and successful organization. Now, take this same approach and engage your peers within the leadership and key-stakeholder levels of your organization and brainstorm best practice ideas and actions that have worked in previous professional experiences and employment to raise universal awareness among everyone that talent is THE essential factor to success and a competitive edge.

Generating a greater understanding throughout your organization as to how much work is involved in finding, attracting, onboarding, retaining, growing and exiting talent is an involved awareness endeavor. The associated time, energy and money involved in the talent life cycle is staggering when you quantify it; not to mention, the concentrated quality time involved in creating a fully functioning intelligence among individuals and the alignment of values, vision, work ethic and dedication.

Awareness of the eleven stages of the ACHIEVEMENT talent process must be owned at the senior-most level and instilled within everyone, and at every level, throughout the organization. The volume of case studies in private sector businesses, non-profit industries, association marketplaces, government agencies and the military of second-level leaders imploding the talent matrix for self-serving needs and aligning data to mislead senior leaders is never ending and sad. The number of rising stars that are run away from organizations routinely, to become human capital for others, is a staggering billion-dollar loss annually and globally.

All things being even, any deliverable a business creates or provides, can be replicated, imitated or advanced by any other business. The market equalizer and differentiator for success today and tomorrow, is the human capital one has on their team and that one can access, partner and collaborate with in the future. To this end, smart leaders and organizations have ingrained in everyone to be on the lookout for any great human capital in the marketplace who could benefit an organization and to look for ways to align and onboard them to your organization – always find a place within your organization for great TALENT!

CAUTION – The one dominant variable that can erode the efficacy of the ACHIEVEMENT talent process will be individual EGOs that stand in the way of growth, development, and success. Due in part, if not whole, to their envy, deceit, and jealousy of others' potential wins.

Individuals within an organization may have varied views of what is Talent and what an organization needs, but your *Values, Vision and Mission Statement* are the glue that can bring everyone back to center. These three ideas serve as the life force for what an organization is, why people would be attracted to it, and even more importantly, communicates to the world what your organization is and is not. When you lose sight of these, the organization becomes everything that it is not and its destiny is never assured or long. These are the organization's commonalities and give talent a reason to be attracted to it; without these you are nothing.

Strong values are the drivers to organizational health. These are the spine of an organization and articulate, communicate and drive what the key stakeholders stand for and engage in. These core Values then drive and inspire the Vision and roadmap that the outside world gauges you off of – Mission Statement.

These are the ingredients that the marketplace sees as your brand and what you tell others you offer, provide, stand for -- or in another word – Brand Promise.

A key aspect of TALENTification is the responsibility of every supervising manager and hiring manager to be cognizant of what each person on their team does, what their growth goals are, and what roles you see that person growing into within the organization. These must also be communicated to the employee.

Talent gaps, lacks and losses should be at a minimum if the ACHIEVEMENT process is at work. Learning of an impending employee departure to pursue employment growth opportunities with another employer — — because an employee did not see themselves within your organization or because you failed to articulate your strategic plans, which included them -- is a failure of the TALENTification succession process.

Human Resource Inclusion
This text does not take into account the obvious HR constraints , individual HR Employee Handbook or Standards-of-Conduct policies.
What this book does address are best-practice ideas and a chronological flow for building a better organization in respect to human capital and talent management.

Individuals, likewise, should be aware of the TALENTification process, as well, and feel comfortable communicating with their supervising manager, hiring manager and/or senior leaders regarding their goals/aspirations and whether they feel those are being met.

Business/C-Suite leaders at their respective levels must architect out their immediate, intermediate and long-term talent needs, growth migration patterns of personnel and the ongoing professional development needs for their business enterprise to survive and thrive – including both the technician skills/aptitudes requirements and the professional KSAs to perform the TDR expected.

The degree of culture disruption, productivity disruption and profitability hits an organization takes due to these failures is massive on an annual and global basis. Architect out individual player aspirations for positional efficiency, productivity, profitability and development as it relates to the individual ... align this with succession needs.

Remember, the overall employee experience is shaped and determined by how you (individually and organizationally) manage your side of each of the ACHIEVEMENT life cycle phases and what the individual employee receives, sees, observes, and internalizes as their EXPERI-ENCE along the way. Every touchpoint from the organization, whether intentional or unintentional, whether overt or not, still shapes the experience an individual has within the work environment. It is clichéd, but always recognize one bad apple (peer or supervisor) can ruin an organization; it takes massive amounts of work to make greatness, and yet, it can be imploded by one simple person.

This experience will be shaped, cultivated and enhanced by how each person plays and executes their roles ... **TALENTification also requires specific roles of its human capital, or talent pool:**

1. Senior Leaders (EDP Level) own the Vision and are the Macro architects;

2. HR Hiring Managers & Talent Management Personnel (LDP Level) own the roles of Ambassadors, Educators & Accountability Compliance Partners;

3. Supervising Managers (MDP Level) serve as the frontline Implementation and serve as the Executors, Developers, and Coaches;

4. Personnel/Employees at large have the responsibility of being Advocates, Participants and Influencers at all levels in embracing the ACHIEVEMENT model process;

5. Outsourced Partners must assume the associated roles that they are engaged to fulfill within the ACHIEVEMENT process, whether that is serving in the role of execution, compliance or accountability partners;

6. Vendor/Service Partners should also be acquainted with the organization's TALENTification ACHIEVEMENT process in order to assist in their best-practice abilities and where applicable; and

7. All KSA development initiatives and professionals carrying out Organizational Development, Training or Educational endeavors must ensure that what they do, in any format or distribution channel, is in alignment with the TALENTification process and strengthens the ACHIEVEMENT process, whatever its specific micro role may be.

As you undertake this important first phase of the ACHIEVEMENT life cycle, always stay focused on how this applies to the TALENT throughout other applications. For an organization, it demands the understanding of each application and how they actually must align as one for ultimate ROI.

The International Labor Relations 2019 study brought forth data that additionally makes the case for strong diversity among your organizational labor force:

First: A Diverse workforce leads to 59% greater innovation over atypical homogenous work groups.

Second: Consumer interest and demand of your organization and goods increases by more than 37%, when diversity exists within and throughout an organization

Mckensey 2020 research study shows dramatic impact on bottom line profitability:

First: 25% increase when there is gender diversity among the Executive Teams

Second: 35% increase when there ethnicity diversity among the Executive Teams

However, same studies in both organizations show a dramatic implosion when organizations force a dramatic change among the Executive Team and it is deemed that the individuals are not net better than their predecessors

Identify at each of the following five TALENT considerations what you expect the new talent to do, i.e., TDR. This must be done first because it leads into the next crucial step: what KSAs are required to perform the role (TDR) you plan to put them in:

1. TALENT management of the INDIVIDUAL;
2. TALENT management of career PATHWAYS;
3. TALENT management of critical essential POSITION pathways;
4. TALENT management of secondary support POSITIION pathways; and
5. TALENT management of the ORGANIZATION

Understanding the life cycle of TALENTification is critical and we hope this book helps synthesize what we know about human capital while providing a simplified approach for individuals and organizations to move beyond the carousel of the past.

Chapter Two

Clarify DEI(A) Identification Of Needs

Clarification & Identification of Needs – With the "Awareness" in hand via DEI talent audits, what do you expect the new talent to do, i.e., what are the Tasks you expect them to perform, what Duties will they have, and what Responsibilities will they have **(TDR)**. This must be done first because it leads into the next crucial step: what KSAs are required to perform the role (TDR) you plan to put them in. There is nothing new here regarding TDR and KSA. What is new, is our focus on executing these two things to perfection. You must be deliberate, objective, and relentless in doing both of these thoroughly, as everything for successful Talentification follows from this. Having the right roles, with the correct TDRs tied to the business strategy, leads you to finding the right people with the right KSA. Also, this must be done with a short-term/long-term view. You are clearly trying to satisfy immediate, near-term requirements, but you must also be cognizant of the future so the talent you bring in can grow with the organization over time.

Recognize that diversity is not just about female versus male or black versus white, it is more importantly about the experiences, abilities, insights and wisdom that a diverse talent pool brings in addressing needs and seeing potential derailments and opportunities within the organization.

Key Performance Indicators **(KPIs)**: *Analytics of Positional Needs and the corresponding competencies associated with each trait/task deliverable needed for effective execution of Positional Needs; Constituents' Buy-In levels; Task v. Traits Analysis Needs, Core Skill Requirements v. Acceptable; What is a Subject-Matter Expert by function/position/strategic levels; Planning; Forecasting of Human-Capital Needs against Positions, Organizational, Market, Growth, P&L, and Attrition Management needs; Utilizing the Player Capability Indexing Model™ to objectively assess talent; SWOT Timelines of Now v. Future; Talent life cycle by Position, Tenure, Individual Aspirations, Organizational Needs, Market Needs and Attrition Needs; Identification of applicable social-style, personality-style and capacity-style assessment instruments and how those analytics reveal compatibility of individuals with the organization, specific teams and overall brand; Etc.*

Let me say this again. With the "Awareness" in hand from talent audits, what do you expect the new talent to do? Now it is time to clearly clarify what are the TDR and KSAs of the role you plan to put them in. There is nothing new here regarding TDR and KSA, what is new is our focus on executing these two things to perfection. You must be deliberate, objective, and relentless in doing both of these steps thoroughly, as everything required for successful Talentification follows from this. Having the right roles, with the correct TDRs tied to the business strategy, leads you to finding the right people with the right KSAs. Also, this must be done with a short-term/long-term view. You are clearly trying to satisfy immediate and near-term requirements, but you must also be cognizant of what the future holds for talent so the talent you bring in can grow with the organization over time.

KPIs include: *Analytics of Positional Needs and then the corresponding competencies associated with each trait/task deliverable needed for effective execution of Positional Needs; Constituents Buy-In levels; Task v. Traits Analysis Needs; Core Skill Requirements v. Acceptable; What is a Subject-Matter Expert by function/position/strategic levels; Planning; Forecasting of Human-Capital Needs against Positions, Organizational, Market, Growth, P&L, and Attrition Management needs; Utilizing the Player Capability Indexing Model to objectively assess talent; SWOT Timelines of Now v. Future; Talent life cycle by Position, Tenure, Individual Aspirations, Organizational Needs, Market Needs and Attrition Needs; Identification of applicable social-style, personality-style and capacity-style assessment instruments and how those analytics reveal compatibility of individuals with the organization, specific teams and over-all brand; Etc.*

Before an organization or individual begins the process of looking at talent as it relates to the people one knows, has on their teams and may come into contact with outside of the organization, start by looking at talent void of human beings. The ability to objectively clarify what talent is, what talent needs you have and what talent means as it relates to the positional functioning necessary to even operate, is a major demarcation from how most everyone presently addresses talent conversations.

I had a client discussion one time, the Board of an east Coast college, student enrollment of about 20,000 students, a an unexpected challenge that arose from how the new President 8-months into their role was causing strife. They hired (on paper) a phenomenal new President, that in short order had replaced the entire executive team with people that really looked just like they did. This drew undue attention, challenges and then a series of rapid turn-over.

In discussion it became evident that the new President had pushed the diversity variable so far into an opposite direction, it had become very distracting to all of their good qualities and goals for the institution. While the new Executive Team representing a student population of 40% black and 52% female, 48% white, 12% Asian, Hispanic and India figuratively, the Executive Team became 100% black and 80% female.

It is always important to discuss and remind everyone of the math to diversity, as we shared in earlier portions of this book.

It is always important to establish the rules of engagement for any bad-actors that may want to pop-up and take advantage of your initiatives. If you're a low performer, you're not a low performer because of your "diversity", it's because you lack the Knowledge, Skills or Abilities or you have a low performer Attitude, Work Ethic or Habit pattern (aka playing the "V" victim card) that must be called out.

This Clarification and Identification of needs is a critical starting point in the TALENTification process and requires specific roles of its human capital, or talent pool. This is owned by and must be thoroughly vetted and executed by level two and three below:

1. Senior Leaders (EDP Level) own the Vision and Macro architects;

2. HR Hiring Managers & Talent Mgt. Personnel (LDP Level) own the roles of Ambassadors, Educators & Accountability Compliance Partners;

3. Supervising Managers (MDP Level) serve as the frontline Implementation Executors, Developers, Coaches;

4. Personnel/Employees at large have the responsibility of being Advocates, Participants and Influencers at all levels in embracing the ACHIEVEMENT Model process;

5. Outsourced Partners must assume the associated roles that they are engaged to fulfill within the ACHIEVEMENT process, whether that is serving in the role of execution, compliance or accountability partners; and

6. Vendor/Service Partners, should also be acquainted with the organization's TALENTification ACHIEVEMENT process to assist in best-practice abilities where applicable.

Analytics of Positional Needs and then the corresponding competencies associated with each trait/task deliverable needed for effective execution of Positional Needs: Start first by performing the flowing exercise. It is important to start here and have a clear, quantifiable matrix of the Knowledge, Skills, Attributes/Abilities, etc. as scoped into the architecture of a Position/Job Statement. Then, in clarifying and identification work of a position from a technician work product, map out the pathway of how that position connects to the positions that proceed and follow said position within the organization.

There are outside and independent organizations that do this for a business, trade associations with benchmark templates, online assessments and analytics available for you to consider and use. Whatever resource you use, ensure that you don't get so fixated on the analytics of the position that you forget the important aspect of this talent conversation – competency.

The data you come up with here is critical to the talent life cycle process, *as it will drive how you find, get and keep essential talent.* It will also clarify how you engage, onboard, develop and look at the entire talent succession process.

Whether you are old school and write it out or you are new school and systematize and make it electronic, it does not matter. What must be defined for each individual role, function, job, position, activity is a line-by-line identification of "tasks" that must be executed. And for each individual "task," a corresponding "competency(s)" expected to do that role, function, job, position, activity must be had. Here is where talent gets derailed; traditionally, significant effort is placed on crafting detailed role, function, job, position, activity "performance descriptions or position statements" for talent to perform and to be able to execute, but little to no real KPIs are attached to each task.

Think of it this way, create your assessment document with the analytics you need and graph it out.

<u>Task/Duty/Responsibility (TDR) Knowledge/Skill/Ability (KSA)</u>

_____

_____

_____

_____

_____

_____

_____

_____

_____

Now this may seem obvious to many, and yet, this is a fundamental mistake made by most. This drill down on every position or task functioning within an organization will drive what your talent life cycle is all about. Imagine an effective misstep here; it will impact adversely how you search for, acquire, onboard, train, resource and support people and initiatives and, in the end, you will have a very complacent and mediocre output as a norm. The answers are most important, as they also drive real-time training, ongoing shaping, and long-term ascension of the best and right talent in the best and right roles.

The importance of the right side corresponding "competency" is that each identified line item will also reveal what the previous "competency" must be and the level of proficiency maintained in it and the level necessary.

Constituent Buy-In Levels: This is where the rubber meets the road. The understanding and buy-in from the leadership level to the participant level is critical here and research of super-achieving and excelling organizations illustrates this. Having truly vetted, proven, credentialed Subject-Matter Experts serving as talent development will be essential to ROI gained or lost. Having the understanding and buy-in from leaders will impact all aspects of your business plans. This is a critical stage in the talent life cycle, as the constituents' buy-in, or lack thereof, WILL impact the talent life cycle and ROI to an organization now and in the future. Here are some of the derailments that can happen to the talent life cycle when constituent buy-in is low, missing or passive-aggressive derailment behaviors are allowed to manifest:

1. If any constituent in the process has personal agendas that are contrary to the health of the organization, they can derail the ultimate stability and health of an organization.

2. If any constituent in the process has personal prejudices that are contrary to the health of the organization, they can derail the ultimate stability and health of an organization.

3. If any constituent in the process is engaged in cronyism that is contrary to the health of the organization, they can derail the ultimate stability and health of an organization.

4. If any constituent in the process is engaged in development and truly is not a credentialed, certified or quantifiably proven

Subject-Matter Expert, the health of the organization will be adversely impacted and the lingering ramifications can become generational.

With constituent buy-in you will see people advocating for one another and championing success. You will see support and inclusion in times of challenge, crises or when there are labor issues. You will see an environment inclusive of your Values, Vision and Mission Statement at every level within the organization.

There is a wide array of constituents to be mindful of in the talent process:

1. The constituents at the Executive or Ownership levels;
2. Constituents in each managerial/leadership role, who can serve as gatekeepers of progress or derailment; and
3. Constituents that have, maintain or control access to resources, capital, decision-making, personnel, etc. If they are not in line with talent initiatives or feel excluded, they can, in fact, create tremendous chaos and derailment.

Remember, at this second phase of TALENTification, we are not evaluating your current human capital or people you may know by name for consideration to be onboarded into your organization, here we are separating the analysis of people from the raw data points that make your organization relevant.

Design or access industry talent audits of what KSAs are minimum sets for every functioning position, job, task, duty in your organization. If there are gaps in the data analytics, then pull together only your super achievers in each role or position for their insights in creating your audit inventory. You can approach your talent audit templates as if you were creating a "certification" process for each position, duty or task. Ask and answer what would be the minimum and maximum KSAs you would set for each. This can give you baselines for performance.

Task v. Traits Analysis Needs, Core Skill Requirements v. Acceptable: As we just discussed, the understanding and identifying of core competencies and correct behaviors in executing tasks, roles, functions, jobs is critical. Having the right people in the right place at the right time is what effective business dynamics is all about. Now, recognizing what the core functions are and what the sequencing is of those jobs is next in the talent life cycle.

Now imagine we take the same matrix just developed and we added a simple assessment index to both sides. Think of it this way, create your assessment document of the analytics you need and graph it out. On the left side would be a score as it relates to any individual you were to assess into the model and on the right side would be the organization's assessment of acceptance of a candidate or employee in any given position:

Position

Candidate	Task/Duty/Responsibility (TDR)	Knowledge/Skill/Ability (KSA)	Organization
1-3-5			1-3-5
1-3-5			1-3-5

1-3-5			1-3-5
1-3-5			1-3-5
1-3-5			1-3-5
1-3-5			1-3-5
1-3-5			1-3-5
1-3-5			1-3-5
1-3-5			1-3-5
1-3-5			1-3-5
1-3-5			1-3-5
1-3-5			1-3-5
1-3-5			1-3-5
1-3-5			1-3-5
1-3-5			1-3-5

Once a grid is created for any "position" within an organization that talent is to populate, you score the importance of the specific "competency TDR" required with either a score of:

1 = Not Important

3 = Required/Expected Proficiency

5 = Mastery Expected

Once the grid is created and scored, then you can use it as an objective template for interviewing outside or inside talent. Their score directly impacts how you can proceed with a person in a current position or future and new positions. This creates a clear road map for talent integration, development, etc. So, if you have someone or hire someone that scores low on the "candidate" side for what you have as an "organization" scored a high-need level, you now know at the outset what you must do to set that candidate and the organization up for success or precisely where failure will become apparent.

As you look at the talent life cycle and how you grow and develop people, recognize that talent knowledge, application and learning must be designed and delivered to grow competencies. First, there is a psychological flow and, second, there is a chronological flow that must be established and followed.

What is a Subject-Matter Expert by function/position/strategic levels: Talent life cycle success is based upon internal and external identification of real, true, battle-tested Subject-Matter-Experts (SME). Engaging a real expert allows you to quantifiably accelerate your rate of failure and success. A real expert serves as a force multiplier to you.

As you explore the knowledge and experience sets needed to master success within your organization and to grow future talent for a strong organization at every level, make sure that a candidate's resume doesn't just boast great titles, but that they actually have a performance record to match.

Create a partnership and mentor under a subject-matter expert. Learn from a true achiever who has spent years, if not decades, accumulating their expertise and from whom you can leverage and learn from within days, weeks or months. In today's robust internet world, with our need for immediate consumption, the depth of subject-matter experts and apparent influencers is astonishing. It is like a kiddie pool of true intellect, understanding, experience and credibility. Yet, most people seem to either be oblivious or complacent.

Today, what passes for an expert or person of legitimate credentials, would have ten years ago been called a "new hire", a "beginner" or a "neophyte." With the aging Baby-Boomer population and entrance of the Millennials and Generation Z rapidly overtaking the majority of the workforce over the next five years, it is estimated that nearly sixty percent of those in managerial/leadership and "boss" positions in 2001 will be retired and gone by 2020.

Generations of Americans were reared with cultural mantras such as work hard, apply yourself, always learn, have self-respect, achieve, help others, operate from etiquette, and you will be rewarded. This created a DNA of what being an AmeriCAN was all about. Today, we have a generational and cultural mindset of "reward me first and maybe I'll work hard." In an ever-exploding rhetoric-infused world, and with this magnitude of loss in experience, intellectual capacity and wisdom, you need to be careful not to become a pawn in someone else's game. The wave of current and impending *self-proclaimed experts* to emerge and attempt to influence the trajectory direction of the future on the world marketplace and in your front yard is here.

With the rise of self-proclaimed experts and wannabes, make sure you cover your actions and are a good steward of others. Consider the company you keep and the company you hire. Therefore, consider these simple vetting observations and questions to unearth the real expert from the self-proclaimed:

1. Have they ever done it as an apprentice or beginner? Can they prove it?

2. Have they ever done it as a journeyman or employee/member?

3. Have they ever done it as a master or leader?

4. Can they prove anything based upon fact, data and logic versus emotion, rhetoric and assertions?

5. What would ten of their reputable clients/benefactors say about their deliverables?

6. Is there a degree in their area of specialty and, if so, do they have it?

7. Is there a trade association certification in their area of specialty and, if so, do they have it?

8. Have they ever been featured in a credible third-party publication or newswire about their specialty?

9. Have they ever penned a White Paper on their specialty?

10. If appropriate, have they ever authored a book that was published by a credible and reputable publisher?

11. Have they ever designed, written, implemented and taught an instruction course in which they are a self- proclaimed expert?

12. Do they hold a patent, trademark or a copyright certificate on their body of work, expertise or deliverable?

13. Are they the innovator of anything in their subject matter, or are they an imitator of others' work?

14. Have they ever spoken before a body of peer experts in their space?

15. If I go to their website, will it prove they are professional?

16. And above all, Can They Prove It?

A major cancer that limits organizations and in many cases will lead to implosions, is having false SMEs in our talent mix. And here is where you really accelerate catching a self-proclaimed expert wannabe in the act of B.S. This will influence your trajectory towards failure and ultimate derailment:

1. Fact-check their resume. If they do not have one, that may be a major clue.

2. Check to see if they have harvested others' credentials and bodies of work as their own. This screams "fraud."

3. Check the social media world for profiles and begin the process of reverse reading. You can add more content to the social media world to bury past trails, but it is very difficult to make data disappear. If their employment changes with the seasons, you need evidence for why they are not a charlatan. If they have quotes for lack of performance that seem to keep coming up in different places and times, then the lack of performance ROI is probably them and not other factors, as reported or cited.

4. Check the credentials, pedigree, and experiences cited and make sure the math adds up.

5. Ask for several references. If they hesitate or can't provide plural references from both the present and the past, this is a major red flag – run.

6. A major clue you are in the presence of a self-proclaimed expert who can't sustain an ROI will be their resistance, or persistent deflection to other topics and the degrading of others to avoid accountability.

7. If you are in an interviewing process situation, consider asking the candidate for copies of the past employer/employee performance reviews for discussion or a copy of their most recent tax statement – these are major reality checks.

Accountability matters in your talent life cycle of subject-matter experts. And how you create or abdicate accountability is critical. Hold on for the pushback when you are in the presence of a self-proclaimed expert as you will see a life cycle of the following:

1. Culture (generational, ethnicity, regional, diversity, etc.) will be rewritten to justify their outcome with no sense of personal ownership or personal responsibility;

2. Values will be abdicated;

3. Deflection (deflect responsibility and blame someone else) away from themselves and the core matter by playing the blame game to make someone else the problem and positioning themselves as the victim.

TALENTification performance success creates clear mandates and dictates. The ramifications of actions, accountability or lack of accountability on you and others, now and later, when influenced by a self-proclaimed expert is devastating. Success achievers will not stay within an organization that maintains and sustains this environment of people. So, if you are that self-proclaimed expert, you may want to really do something meaningful, contribute something meaningful, and get a job. If you have never done anything, don't proclaim to have done so – step aside and let the real innovators/adults lead the way!

Engaging a real expert allows you to quantifiably accelerate your rate of success. A real expert serves as a force multiplier for you. Engage a sage as a coach for daily or weekly check-ins and accountability growth opportunities. Identify mentors to develop and guide your growth. Create peer groups that are comprised of people with greater credentials than you to serve as a 360° benchmark for excellence in all that you do. Develop a balanced IQ and EQ with substantial readings and continuous mental DNA enrichments on a regular basis. And, explore all opportunities to mentally tithe to others – but only those that will appreciate you and pay it forward.

Just as complacency and mediocrity grows contempt, so too can success beget success in your talent life cycle.

SWOT (Strength, Weaknesses, Opportunities, Threats) Timelines of Now v. Future; Talent life cycle by Position, Tenure, Individual Aspirations, Organizational Needs, Market Needs and Attrition Needs: Applying fundamental business lessons to everything one does within the talent life cycle process is critical. So is the alignment of what an organization needs to be vibrant and the people within it now and those that are onboarded in the future.

With every individual, there is a point at which a person in a position is ready to progress onward and, if that is not met, then the performance declines and the organization is harmed. Additionally, some people, even great people, will not be long termers for an organization and will depart at certain timelines in their career pathway. So, the talent life cycle must be cognizant of this and plan for it. Just as the talent life cycle owns talent succession planning, it should know years in advance when someone is coming up to their exit date or retirement, and have already created a strong bench of worthy internal candidates to assume that opening and opportunity.

Again, remember, here at the second of the eleven elements of the ACHIEVEMENT Model, it is all about CLARIFICATION of Talent Needs. The answers here can be collected by evaluating not actual people (we will do a deeper dive on people later), but the analytics of roles, functions, positions, and task accomplishment.

To begin this drill down work, let's think of a schematic or organizational diagram, void of people, of any organization. You would have your C-Suite and Board at the top, with lines of accountability connecting each identified spot, again void of actual first-person names. No matter the size of an organization, you can scale this up or down. Let's plot big for discussion; let's go Fortune 100 in size for scope and clarity. Under each C-Suite you would have core business practices and subsequent support functionaries to each spot identified above. As you build downward on this organizational diagram, you will eventually arrive at front-line functionaries for each line and the number of slots/positions under each that would be required for you to be market relevant today and tomorrow. Tomorrow is important for this lesson because if your tomorrow will illuminate fewer people or more people in your diagram, then the concept of talent life cycle comes into play: where do the people you have go and where do you find future people?

When looking at the people component and what data that can reveal for effective talent life cycle considerations, always identify the actual rockstar who others would benchmark off of rather than the most tenured person in a role.

A powerful means to objectively identifying the human capital needed to efficiently address or excel at the TDR, is the utilization of the Player Capability Indexing Model. The utilization of this model leads into the next crucial step: what KSAs are required to perform the role (TDR) you plan to put them in. This model can be used as an overlay to any Job/Position Statement, talent opening announcement, Personnel Performance Evaluation system or Interviewing session, etc.

There are several generally accepted human resource modeling formulas that can be used to scope needs within the SHRM or Association Talent Development (formerly ASTD), and whether you use Root Cause Analysis™, Human Performance Improvement™ modeling, or the Player Capability Indexing model, you need a clear road map.

Over the past four decades, through working with clients including global Fortune 100 Firms to mid-cap entrepreneurial businesses, NASA, DoD, the National Guard, Farm Credit Services banking groups and a wide range of non-profit and evangelical institutions, we have learned that understanding the human-capital talent as a formula is essential to understanding TALENTification. From my coaching and consulting work with individuals such as billionaire entrepreneurs, corporate executives, military generals, professional athletes, celebrities, musicians and politicians, we have learned that understanding the human-capital talent as a formula is essential to understanding TALENTification model, process and DNA.

Your ability to understand objectively within yourself and others the depth of what talent means, is essential. One way by which this can be assessed, quantified and leveraged is through the use of the Player Capability Indexing Model. Each letter in the formula represents the operational DNA of your human capital. Each letter represents what it takes to fully understand the KSA and TDR of business and talent. Each letter represents the indexing of how to assess what an individual brings with them; where their gaps and deficiencies are; and how to calibrate the entire talent life cycle and all human-capital integration for one overall, effective organization. Understanding this formula will serve you in the talent life cycle at multiple steps in the ACHIEVEMENT flow.

The *Player Capability Indexing Model*™ as a formula:

$$C = (T2+A+P+E+C) \ E2 \ x \ R2 = R$$

1. **R = Results.** Starting on the right side of the equation, the last letter in the formula represents Results: any output or ROI

desired. In order get to that R, you must objectively and thoroughly understand the chemistry or what we call the operational DNA of an individual, each of the letters inside of the parenthesis and what each represents. To do this indicates you have an objective and thorough understanding of the C at the opposite left side of the equation.

2. **C = Capability.** Capability is the driver of talent that enables significant results to be continuously generated. The greater the depth of any and every subsequent letter enables the Results. Conversely, for the complacent among us, it is their diminished desire to not draw upon any lettered capability driver nor their desire to add any real-time relevant depth to any lettered category that serves as the cancer to the talent cycle. So, the letters within the parenthesis drive the Capability level.

3. **T2 = Training.** As represented by any deliverable of knowledge, whether formal or informal education, technical or non-technical education, certification driven or simply on-the-job knowledge acquisition. The number two adjacent to the T simply reminds you of two applications of the T. One is for total T gained from birth to the present. So T1 is Past Training and gives you a snapshot of the talent as it is presently. The T2 would be for Future training need:, how you continue to engage and grow talent within the organization to meet daily work product needs and future opportunities. Superstars and loyal engaged members of any organization are always seeking more T acquisition.

4. **A = Attitude.** One that projects a winner and not a whiner. Assessment of talent, here, can be measured through work ethic,

dedication, commitment to organization and others; willingness to contribute; passion; execution; and a host of other KPIs.

5. **P = Performance.** This is reflective of past accomplishments, performance-records, participation, leadership and follower positions that would serve as a mental imprint of self-belief and awareness of what can be done. Ability to execute at desired performance levels provides talent analytics on how to keep one engaged and what the pathway is for continued success.

6. **E = Experiences.** From birth to present, experiences are enormous windows through which talent reveals itself and from which one can draw strategically from for Results. This imprint will also reveal developmental opportunities and needs to grow healthy talent within an organization. What have been and are their DEI influencers and shapers that calibrates their experience orientation.

7. **C = Culture.** Cultural awareness and upbringing also calibrate performance and self-worth, what you know you can draw upon, what you know you can manage. But what you fail to recognize may be the driver of results or implosion. Culture drives talent, so remember Culture is a wide range of influencers, which at this stage serves to give you valuable insights prior to hiring and onboarding an individual. It also provides you with insights as to how you are calibrating your organization. Culture drivers include, but are not limited to: Generational Segmentation, Ethnicity, Social-Economic Positioning, Education, Gender, Politics, Lifestyle, Religion, Geography, and many more.

8. **E2 = Expectations.** Calibrate what really shows up as talent or lack of talent. The first interpretation of E is yours. How you see yourself calibrates whether you bring your A Game or B Game

to the show. And the second E is the other person's E of you. Knowing the two and calibrating them together allows for aligned effectiveness.

Expectations that are not aligned are the top reasons for implosions of human capital.

There are three KPIs that must be understood by all interacting parties or you will be out-of-alignment and the toxicity that will grow from this will become cancerous to the individuals and organization.

First: You want to share Expectation-of-Position/Job and solicit feedback of their understanding and expectations of same!

Second: You want to share Expectation-of-Organization and solicit feedback of their understanding and expectations of same!

Third: You want to share your Personal-Expectations of them and solicit feedback of their understanding and expectations of same/you!

9. **R2 = Relationships.** Those that a person has had in their life, thus the first interpretation of the R is past tense in nature, serves as a distinct calibrator and multiplier to the entire formula and that is how talent leverages everything. Sadly, for far too many today, their talent energy is snuffed out because of the ever-increasing circle of negative influencers and stimulants around them. From a talent development perspective, onboarding sequencing and mentor assignments, etc., will be the future Relationships that can be aligned with an individual to shape their future, the second interpretation of the R.

In working to create a greater organization of diversity of talent and thought, energy of inclusion and participation, and equity in participation, advancement and compensation may critically mean you have to be very purposeful in the future Relationships one is exposed into and participates with.

The clarification and identification of needs before you introduce actual personalities into the talent mix, is critical to really building a universally successful enterprise. Using a model like the Player Capability Indexing Model will prove a meaningful instrument for scoping the talent needs of any endeavor and provide valuable insight into each of the following ACHIEVEMENT talent stages.

Let me share one reflective past tense way to apply PERFORMANCE in considering the hiring, promotion or accepting a transfer of an individual to your team or organization. I am reminded of an individual I had interactions with, as he moved from rank-to-rank in the United States Army National Guard. In his career he had moved from a New England area State to a major Southwest State and ultimately to DC. In his military career he had always left his command in worse shape than it was when he arrived and he had failed at every leadership role he ever held, yet his Officer Evaluation Reports never reflected this. You want to dig into anyone purported accomplishments/performances and really ensure that if they are being presented to you as a winner, do some major research to ensure you are not inheriting someone else's bad luggage or a person hat is a smooth talker, relationship builder and toxic disaster in waiting!

This Player Capability Indexing Model can also be used to engineer the career development and pathway development of individuals within an organization. Used as an overlay to an individual's real-time talent, as defined by each variable in the model, you can then plot out next developmental actions in each variable as it relates to your organization and the individual being assessed. These variables can be benchmarked against actual Job Description needs for an objective engagement by talent professionals within an organization or those brought in as outside consultants by an organization to engineer success.

This second phase of the ACHIEVEMENT Model is critical. At this phase, you are working without a specific person in mind. What you are doing here is designing success on an individual basis and as a linked step in designing pathways for human-capital development, pathways of vocations, pathways of careers, or pathways of the life cycle of your human capital.

This is the step that most organizations fail at the most. They work from outdated documents and analytics, or even worse, allow inexperienced, ill-trained or, in some organizations I have consulted with, massively failed individuals to perform the data development... The better the analytics are at evaluating and designing the work product output needed, the more detailed and real-time Job Descriptions you can craft.

In many organizations today, lean teams and maxed out leaders fall behind in keeping clear, current analytics (update Job Descriptions) for achieving talent performance standards and future forecast of talent needs. In order to solve this problem, organizations can always have the rockstar in any position provide updated and real-time data points into these previous models, as to what is really necessary to perform a duty, role, job, etc. at rockstar super-achiever status. Have each Job Description/Fit-for-Duty statement reviewed and updated on a regular basis; then you will never find yourself in a position of a major, organization-wide, Job Description and position pathway remapping.

Rule of Three - In every endeavor at this level, benchmark your analytics against three core documents. I believe these three items should be interlinked and used in concert at every level within your TALENTification process:

1. *Employee Handbook* – Or whatever you call this resource. Everything your organization values, expects, demands and will not tolerate should be documented here, so everyone knows the rules of the game for engagement within your organization.

2. *Job Description* – Should be as detailed as appropriate for clarity of work product performance, with all KPIs detailed as necessary.

3. *Performance Assessment/Evaluation* – Everything that is detailed in a Job Description should also be detailed on the Performance Review. All items should be in alignment with your Employee Handbook.

Each of these three documents should be aligned for peak talent assessment, acquisition, onboarding and retention.

The core stakeholders charged with ensuring an organization has the talent to fulfill today's brand promises and needs, as well as to ensure the proper internal development of talent to be market ready for any tomorrow needs, must own this critical obligation. Mapping out the

1. Talent pathway for the development of every member within an organization;

2. The pathway of core competencies necessary to excel within a position;

3. The pathway of how positions link horizontally and vertically within the business enterprise area or the organization overall is critical; and

4. The pathway for positions is essential for ACHIEVEMENT!

The pathway architecture, in and of itself, is a profession and this is critical to the talent discussion and human-capital management for an organization – both for immediate operational realities and in building the succession success of any organization.

Remember, the overall employee experience is shaped and determined by how you (individually and organizationally) manage your side of each of the ACHIEVEMENT life cycle phases and what the individual employee receives, sees, observes, and internalizes as their EXPERIENCE along the way. Every touchpoint from the organization, whether intentional or unintentional, whether overt or not, still shapes the experience an individual has within the work environment.

Now, let's take everything you have just read and force-multiple it to be relevant over your horizon. We will discuss Radical Relevance® towards the end of this book and how you ensure that you address you real-time needs, BUT, you must be mindful of what is over your horizon and what you future needs will be that your

TALENTification must already be waiting for. So, when we discuss Clarify DEIIdenification of Needs, this must also be discussed in perspective to your organizations future tense:

- Future in the immediate needs

- Future of intermediate needs

- Future of long term needs

To attain the DEI mix you seek for your organization, if you realize the market place is not producing viable individuals, then hold your market space accountable. An example, if you are finding it difficult to find viable candidates for hire in any demographic, because they lack the Knowledge, Skills, Abilities, Values, Work Ethic, Discipline, Etc., then do the uncomfortable and call it out. Then explore how you can provide a viable solution pathway.

This may be unpopular, but true leaders must occasionally wear their adult pants and demand an adult conversation.

I once interviewed Warran Buffett for my www.ProfessionalPerformanceMagazine.com and I asked him, aside from the obvious financials of a business or market that everyone likes to talk about, what other factor do you look at when making an investment for Berkshire Hathaway, his response is impactful for both this Chapter and the next:

"If the business is going to be labor intense, I believe you have to evaluate the labor pool. IF there are great public K12 schools, a great community college and trade school system, if there are great colleges and universities that feed that area, then we know it will be a winner. A

winner as those schools will continuously produce a diverse and edu-cation population pool!"

As you undertake this important second phase of the ACHIEVE-MENT life cycle, always stay focused on how this applies to the TALENT in a multitude of applications. For an organization, it de-mands the understanding of each application and how they actually must align as one for ultimate ROI. Identify at each of the following five TALENT considerations, what you expect the new talent to do, TDR. This must be done first because it leads into the next crucial step: what KSAs are required to perform the role (TDR) you plan to put them in:

1. TALENT management of the INDIVIDUAL;

2. TALENT management of career PATHWAYS;

3. TALENT management of critical essential POSITION path-ways;

4. TALENT management of secondary support POSITION path-ways; and

5. TALENT management of the ORGANIZATION.

Understanding the life cycle of TALENTification is critical and we hope this book helps synthesize what we know about human capital and provides a simplified approach for individuals and organiza-tions to move beyond the carousel of the past.

Clarifying the DEI needs internally and cultivating those pathways is critical to being a sound business place of choice and in creating a brand that outsiders benchmark off of and want to be associated with. The Player Capability Index (PCI) is an amazingly objective model for increasing your awareness into others and in developing the core and critical KPIs internally throughout your organization (and within your own mindset) to be relevant today and tomorrow.

With that said, the Player Capability Index must be utilized at each level within the ACHIEVEMENT™ process. IT must be held out as a tool for measurement in spot lighting individual efforts for differentiation.

An example; I had a billion-dollar-client that I worked with for a long time, One day the former CHRO (Chief Human Resource Officer) and at the time CAO (Chief Administrative Officer) shared a story ... She had gotten pregnant at an early age, was single, lived on her own. Not to be deterred, she put herself through college, found a great employer that she could dedicate herself into, while working full time. At the time diversity was not too kind for most, for her she blazed her path with discipline, perseverance, professionalism, academia and passion. Today, she absolutely loves what she does and the individuals she gets to work alongside of everyday - A great DEI story!

Chapter Three
Human-Capital Acquisition & DEI(A)

Human-Capital Acquisition – You are now ready to identify where the talent you need is and how to go about recruiting them (internally or externally). Acquiring talent should be a simple multiphased process. You may need to consider the systems you use and the people interactions for finding, interviewing and hiring diverse talent, as sometimes unconscious bias may cause you to miss the best talent in the market place. You may need to consider if your processes intimidate perspective candidates from even applying, and if so develop solutions, include individuals of diversity from within your organization now to provide advise on how to improve your outreach approach and interviewing practices.

Too often we see organizations designing very robust, but convoluted processes, using numerous external search agencies for the same job or talent pool. Simple processes are easy to implement, easy to explain to the organization and hiring manager, and result in quicker placements. A simple but thorough job specification/description is the first step (generated through a coordinated effort of the hiring manager with the human resources manager). Advertising and sourcing should be done through the organization's website, targeted external social media networking portals, and select search firms, i.e. those that have expertise in the domain you are recruiting for. If your organization seems to out-of-balance from a diversity perspective, consider applications that hide contact name and geographical references, so you can focus on actual work experience and abilities to find and vet better candidates.

In attracting, recruiting and retaining diverse talent to your workplace, consider:

- Remove the bias language in the job announcement.
- Set clear salary expectations and negotiation.
- Include flex work options.
- Recruit from many colleges and university to increase applicant pool diversity.
- Use targeted referrals to reach underrepresented groups.
- Recruit experienced candidates who are returning to the workforce.
- Use software to facilitate increased blind interviews.
- Conduct structured interviews of everyone every time, to ensure a consistent baseline of Q&A from every candidate.

- Use skill-based assessments.

- Have people apply with a blind resume, remove any KPis that could trigger unconscious bias in accepting, reviewing or interviewing a candidate.

- Provide diversity resources and training internally as situationally appropriate to level up everyone's abilities.

By deploying these KPIs and others, implicit bias es can be vetted and eliminated in this part of the ACHIEVEMENT process.

There is a classic example of this done by researchers and Orchestra Directors, back in 1970 and it still serves as a wake-up call today, both for us as individuals and our institutions – implicit and inherent biases revealed.

- In this 1970 Orchestra Design Research, the best Orchestra Directors adamantly made the point that they were not bias in hiring performers, they hire for excellence.

- At this time roughly 10% of the musicians were women

- Then a hidden curtain was used for them to interview new future musicians that tried out for new roles, that played from behind that curtain.

- An immediate increase of 40% new musicians were women!

Consider a more global and through outreach for example if you are wanting college graduates, are you establishing communication connections with 100 percent of the institutions in your geography? And, with key contacts and advocates win each of those institutions. Are you possibly creating an Employee Resource Group (ERG) of a diverse cross section of your talent pool and involving them in this first critical step? Recognize from your Human Capital Talent Outlook Report (spreadsheet), that you may need to connect into different venues, locations and individuals to find diversity talent, if it is not within your present networks and outreach initiatives.

KPMG 2030 DEI goal is to have 1/3 of their labor force be from the "working class" and not what they deemed to be their historical model for hiring from the "elite class" in pursuit of being a more inclusive global organization. TO do this, some of their proactive human capital acquisition measures are to be:

- Don't just interview and hire from top tier institutions.

- Limit the # of referral hires.

- Limit top earning household incomes of hires

- Don't make collegiate or professional sports a job hire reason.

Be careful in hiring for too much of a Cultural Fit, that you don't actually create a bias against diversity. There are an endless array of ways to ensure diversity and fit.

While Likeability may be one indicator that draws us together or may be a flashing reason you like and want to add someone to our team, be careful. It should be merely one of many KPIs you use to vet and on-board talent.

First realize that there are trade associations and affinity groups for every demographic and trade one can imagine. As you seek to broaden your view of diversity, reach out to identified demographic representation groups to lean more bout them and share with them what your opportunities are for their span-of-influence.

And as you strive to create a diverse and equitable work environment that embraces inclusion, ensure that those organizations you seek to connect with do the same, if an organizations wishes to operate in this global DEI world than they can't be exclusive of some, at the statement of inclusive to others!

Diversity for the sake of Diversity is not Diversity. It is pure conscious DISCRIMINATION and isolationism – Using the Player capability Index model as an objective tool can allow you to navigate unconscious bias and conscious bias to ensure you find talent, regardless of the diversity and that you grow talent because of diversity, to ensure equity and inclusion for all!

DEI initiatives, programs and stewards should never use this as a weapon of quotas or an instrument to re-write one's perspective of history.

Whether you frame the conversation and management around diversity or community phrasing, equity or merit of contribution, inclusion or opportunity gateways, DEI is the global reality and so too should it be yours.

Consider both **Clarification & Identification of Needs** and **Human-Capital Acquisition** as having to ebb-and-flow back-and-forth with one another to be fluid and effective for your DEI goals … For example, to ensure that Implicit Bias nor Unconscious Bias influence these two critical elements of the ACHIEVEMENT Model, ensure that what you post, how you post, where you post the openings does not drive talent away before you ever meet.

Bias, we have them and that is our individual and organizational reality. This does not make one good nor bad, it just is what it is. With clarity, awareness and understanding you can draw upon tools, analytics, research, dashboards to ensure you do not limit yourself nor your orgianzation.

KPIs: *Designing instruments and pathways for Attracting those Needs (organic, service bureaus, agents, online portals, etc.); Use skill based assessments; Remove language or requirements that may suggest a bias; Use software to facilitate blind interviews; Promotion and Marketing of Needs; Interviewing and Vetting Process/Systems/Instruments to Gain the Appropriate and Best Human Capital Available; Addressing Biases; Ensuring Aspirations of Candidate Prospects match Organization and internal Key Constituents.*

You are now ready to identify objectively what you need, where the talent you need is, and how to go about recruiting it (internally or externally). Acquiring talent should be a simple multi-phased process. Too often we see organizations designing very robust but convoluted processes, using numerous external search agencies for the same job or talent pool. Simple processes are easy to implement, easy to explain to the organization and hiring manager, and result in quicker placements. A simple but thorough job specification/description is the first step (generated through a coordinated effort of the hiring manager with the human resources manager). Advertising and sourcing should be done through the organization's website, targeted external social media networking portals, and/or select search firms, i.e. those that have expertise in the domain you are recruiting for. Designing instruments and pathways for Attracting those Needs (organic, service bureaus, agents, online portals, etc.); Promotion and Marketing of Needs; Interviewing and Vetting Process/Systems/Instruments to Gain the Appropriate and Best Human Capital Available; Addressing Biases;

Ensuring Aspirations of Prospects match to Organization and internal Key Constituents.

Talent acquisition is your lifeblood of success. You are now ready to identify objectively what you need, where to find the talent you need, and how to go about recruiting it (internally or externally). Acquiring talent should be a simple multi-phased process: With clarity of the workflow needs assessed and clarity as to the TDR you expect of the prospective human capital you desire to find, vet and onboard, which will be aligned with the KSAs required to perform the role (TDR) you plan to put them in. Now, let's engage the marketplace for opportunities.

Before you look at the many platforms available to find talent, start internally with your existing employees who already know your enterprise, systems, culture, environment, SOPs, etc., and create a process by which all growth opportunities and new needs are shared internally. Invite your rockstars, who already possess the KSAs you seek, to become your first line of referrals for qualified prospects in your interview process. You can even create a Referral Compensation stream for quality new hires, whereby a bonus (perhaps 50% of total offered bonus) may be provided upon onboarding new talent and the balance referral compensation bonus at a set anniversary date of employment (perhaps at end of successful year one, the balance 50% is paid) to the referring colleague.

This example works to generate quality talent acquisition and creates a culture by which everyone has a vested interest in jointly participating in a new hire's onboarding, and an even greater vested interest (which we will detail in the next chapter) in integrating others for lasting success within the organization.

By creating a team or special advocacy group within your enterprise for seeking out new talent, and even creating a culture where people are always seeking great new talent for the organization, you also access a deeper network of potential great talent by tapping into your colleague's networks, circles, and interactions.

Use the work product from the first two stages of the ACHIEVE-MENT Model to direct you where to go for candidates and to draw upon the analytics to evaluate the human capital you seek. We will defer, on the specific instruments and service organizations that you can engage and online platforms that can be used, to others in the industry.

What we will address is what these accessed resources/people should deliver to you as their final work product, if it is to be of any measurable value to you.

A simple but thorough job specification/description is the first step (generated through a coordinated effort of the hiring manager and the human resources manager). Who will actually be held accountable for the work product of the new hire/talent? It is critical that this individual have skin and brain in the game. They are closest to actual work- product generation of the human capital and they must be involved in the real-time development and updating of the TDRs involved. Amazingly, over our combined decades of experience, most Job Descriptions/Performance Responsibility Statements, or whatever you call these human resource labor documents, are out-dated or flat-out inaccurate.

Sit down with a peak performer in any TDR, your rockstars, and ask them, separate of any Job Descriptions/Performance Responsibility

Statements, what they actually do. You may be stunned at what they write down, as opposed to what the human resources manager may have on file. Then ask them what actual KSAs are required to perform the role (TDR) they are in. Again, you may be stunned at what is revealed as opposed to what the human resources manager, and in many cases, what the actual hiring manager may believe is reality. Many hiring managers are removed from the actual work product (having been a while since they last performed the KSAs of the role) and are simply unaware.

Another consideration in the documents and analytics used to source great candidates to be interviewed and to assist you in the actual interviewing process is whether your documents are focused on the past, present or future. Are they historical snapshots, and therefore outdated documents? Are they a present-tense picture of what individuals are doing on a daily basis to take care of current market needs? Or do these documents contain language and direction reflective of forward-focused future human-capital expectations?

You can create a regular stress test to these documents, in real time, by tasking the hiring manager and human resource manager to gather best practice documents for continuous benchmarking endeavors. Whether you engage in active or passive recruitment, there are a host of options for acquiring great talent. Do not feel as if you must accept whatever you can get. For example:

1. Trade Industry/Associations – If you are a member of any trade association in your industry or to professional positions, leverage them for reference documents that they would use. These can be used to calibrate your own strategic analysis;

2. Competition – If you have a collegial relationship with your industry peer group, request that they share human resource and C-Suite documents for best practice considerations;

3. Academic Journals/Publications/Texts – A trip to your local University or online academic portal will provide you with valuable resources that may contain templates, case studies and anecdotal references for consideration in your documents and talent development trajectories;

4. Performance Assessment/Reviews – Remember the wise saying of what gets measured gets performed? You should place every Job Description/Performance Responsibility Statement next to the Performance Assessment or Review documents and there should be an aligned synergy between each. If you are expecting performance from one document, then that should also be what is evaluated, and visa versa;

5. Common Self Sense – You have seen mis-hires many times in your life. An organization thought they had the perfect candidate and hired them, only to later find that there was a major misalignment between the two and layers of challenges or talent-management problems ensued. Evaluate why that happened and design analytics to guard against this happening routinely in your organization; and

6. Adviser Network – Consider tapping into your advisory board, Board-of-Directors, CEO-to-CEO peer groups, Chambers-of-Commerce or other vetted, proven, been-there-done-that professionals for feedback, guidance and tips from their university-of-hard-knocks experience.

Invest the time upfront and it will produce significantly greater interactions and undertakings all the way through the talent life cycle and this new talent-acquisition phase.

Consider this in the creation of your documents, and thus, analytics: If you want to bring a new level of transparency to what you do in the talent-acquisition process and, later, in the talent management and development phases, place these two documents -- Job Descriptions/Performance Responsibility Statements and Positional Performance Reviews -- in front of the hiring team and the candidate being interviewed and go down them, line by line in your interview process. Evaluate not just what the candidate says per line item, but pay attention to their non-verbal cues, as well. This may be a very valuable exchange and prove very insightful for you in evaluating the candidate for hire or promotion.

Advertising and sourcing should be done through the organization's website, targeted external social media networking portals, and/or select search firms, i.e. those that have expertise in the domain you are recruiting for. Promotion and Marketing of Needs; Designing instruments and pathways for Attracting those Needs (organic, service bureaus, agents, online portals, etc.). The reality is that we live in a global marketplace today. While it will always be valuable to be laser focused in the networks you access to let the greatest possible talent pool know of your openings and opportunities, you don't just want to shotgun your announcement. Rather, you want to announce opportunities on as many diverse communication channels as possible to reach the maximum number of qualified candidates.

Ask yourself some of these questions to identify where to promote your opportunities:

For example:

1. Geography - Where do the great candidates for what I need live? Go there.

2. Online – What websites and social media platforms do my candidates visit? Go there.

3. Who – Who knows this prospect pool? Go there.

4. What – What online employment portals and platforms do my prospective candidates associate with, post onto, search or follow? Be there.

5. Last – Where did your last new hire, rockstar find you or come from? Go there.

Your own organization should be ground zero for any and every acquisition opportunity need and promotion (unless you need to be more strategic and stealthy to replace an existing member of your organization and you do not want to alert someone to their impending demise).

Make it easy for candidates to find information on your website. There should be a "WANT TO JOIN OUR TEAM" area that shares your story with others and the pathway for contacting you for employment inquiry. And if you have a physical plant (or multiple operating locations), there should be a standard go-to place for internal candidates to see new opportunities available within the organization for advancement, transition, lateral or vertical movement, promotion and for outside talent considerations.

This can also serve as a retention opportunity. A person on the team (unbeknownst to you) may be bored with their present work assignment and consider leaving your team. If they see new areas of interest as opportunities, they may now stay and become even more engaged within the organization.

Another area for acquiring great talent is from within your industry. Explore reasons great talent would want to leave your competition and come to you. This exercise may be very revealing. Further, the ability to acquire talent from the marketplace that can be fast-tracked through the onboarding process can also be exceedingly profitable. You can access this talent pool through.

1. Trade Shows – Notice the potential talent right in front of you at trade shows you attend, participate in or display at for interaction opportunities of hidden talent right in front of you.

2. Personal Networks – Look at your personal networks and networking endeavors and recognize if there is talent from the other team in your midst.

3. Subject-Matter Expert On Display – Become more aware of the Subject-matter Expert penning articles in Trade Journals and industry interviews, and individuals you may come across on Podcasts, Blogs, Vlogs, Television.

4. Internal Referral Network, Bounty Program and/or Bonus - Create an internal system by which current employees can make referrals into the organization from their personal network. These fast-tracked prospective candidates if hired, are recognized with an incentive program offering to the internal employee. This could include a cash referral bonus upon hiring a new employee and a bonus payback at that new employee's

successful 6-month anniversary. This would also create a sense of responsibility within the referring current employee to ensure that the new hire is onboarded and set up for success, which plays to the "I" level of the ACHIEVEMENT model of "Integrating Onboarding" of a new, healthy, successful colleague.

5. Human-Capital Staffing/Resourcing Agencies/Online Portals – It is to your advantage to always consider engaging firms that specialize in your specific talent positions or industry for outside human-capital prospect options. Have a clearly defined "Job Description" for what you need and a great Avatar, if possible, defining the ideal new candidate that fits best into your culture, organization and growth needs that can be referenced for finding more candidates for consideration.

Interviewing and Vetting Process/Systems/Instruments to Gain the Appropriate and Best Human Capital Available; Addressing Biases; Ensuring Aspirations of Candidate Prospects match to Organization and internal Key Constituents. Here is where the real work begins. Don't rush this process, as this is what tends to become the reality and where the derailments experienced later in the talent life cycle actually take root. You should prepare for this as if it were the #1 meeting of the year that will make or break your own career and the company's ability to even exist.

Before we talk about the human resource instruments that can be considered for personality style, social style, behavioral tendencies, etc. (DISC, Myers-Brigg, Hogan, Etc,) -- which all can be sourced and utilized as employment instruments to determine the fit and ability to succeed of a candidate before being hired -- let's start with what you know about the prospect, candidate or colleague to be interviewed.

Do you really gain the depth of response required using simple questions? If not, go deeper for greater meaning and predictive analysis, consider some of these ideas for better interviewing:

1. The 5W & 1H Rule – As you evaluate the candidate before meeting them live, run these six power questions and all of the variations of them to determine what level of understanding you have of them. Every vague, generic or non-in-depth response you have now, drives the quality and quantity of questions you need to be asking later ... Create a simple paper template or electronic tracking document to gather the data applicable to the Who, What, When, Where, Why and How ...

2. Research – Look through social media platforms for any accounts that a candidate may have (LinkedIn, as an example, is a great online resume, referral, reference, recommendation, credential portal). Evaluate the picture presented by the candidate; this will provide you with additional talent insight of the person that you may have not known or that may not be revealed in a traditional application process. Also, do a deep dive into what the candidate indicates is their talent as you benchmark their data against the Player Capability Indexing Model I have shared in previous chapters. Evaluate what their accomplishments are, the body of work associated with them and the timelines of their accomplishments.

3. Team Interviews – Consider bringing in your Rock Stars, Evolving Stars and Developing Stars as collaboration partners in

meeting, interviewing and participating in the initial outreach considerations.

4. Situational Real-Time Questions – Pose real-time situation challenges that you are experiencing "in part" to potential new hire or new colleague to your team and have them as a follow-up and prep to a second interview or meeting homework potential solutions.

I once had a senior executive that a client had hired who was failing miserably. When I did a cursory review of their social media presence, I quickly recognized that their accounts had massive contradictions, which indicated a gross misrepresentation of their credentials. This made it easy to see why they were imploding, yet no one had ever done this simple deep dive analysis!

1. Beyond Referrals – The real magic of a candidate's referrals, recommendations or reference list is to evaluate if the people vouching for the candidate are people of stature to start with (Mom and Dad don't count). So evaluate the credentials, stature, rank, and organization names that the candidate has associated with themselves. The real science here is to reflect on whether you know anyone connected to the references provided or who has engaged your candidate previously and vet them through those degrees-of-separation contacts.

2. Team Interview – The people who have a direct vested interest in the candidate's position should be considered for participation in the interviews and interactions for additional post-interview perspective and feedback, observations, and/or a gut check.

3. Templated Questions – While letting the conversation flow and proactively presenting questions accordingly, always make sure that you have core questions at hand to discuss. These questions should be designed to gather insights to benchmark against your talent matrices (Job Descriptions, Performance Reviews, Goals, Budgets, Business Plan needs, Client nuances, etc.). Have real-life anecdotal situations to gather their insights for how they think, act, respond and would address situations. Have a real-time, realistic case study situation that you can present to them. Likewise, create some push questions and scenarios for discussion about the talent pathway or career trajectory onward from this position, to get an early glance into their potential within the organization.

4. Environment – Yes, create an environment conducive for everyone to be comfortable. Spend time walking the environment with the candidate; put them into the work space dynamic, if possible. Discuss this and evaluate what they say, do not say and how they act (body language) as you interact with them and walk them around. This is all valuable insight and data.

5. Job Description – Bring out the actual document you'll use to assess the candidate (if hired) in 30-, 60-, 90 days or at your organization's official (annual) performance review times. Walk and talk through this actual document line-by-line conversationally for understanding and feedback on the tasks that you are potentially asking them to perform.

6. Employee Handbook – Bring out the actual document from which you and your organization will expect the new talent to follow. Talk through this actual document (line-by-line if

necessary) conversationally for understanding and feedback on company culture.

7. Performance Assessment or Review – Bring out the actual document you'll use to assess the candidate, if hired, in 30-, 60-, 90 days or at your organization's determined official (annual) performance review times. Walk and talk through this actual document line-by-line conversationally for understanding and feedback on that which you are potentially asking them to perform.

It is from the pre-work and data you can collect, matched up with the interview and interaction notes, comments, and actions that you'll get a clear picture of the candidate's Values, Vision and Professional Aspirations. Make sure you understand where they have come from and whether their past professional history is in alignment with what they say are their Values/Aspirations. Then ensure your organization's talent needs match up with who they are now and that they match up with where your future talent needs will be. Make sure you evaluate how their Aspirations (goals, expectations, desired accomplishments, career pathway, retirement [whatever that may mean]) are aligned with the organization's.

You should never rush the vetting and hiring process. Consider a series of meetings to give all parties an opportunity to become comfortable with one another. iI is like a courtship: It's always better to break up before you get married. It is always easier to disengage with a candidate during the interview process and much more difficult to eliminate someone after they have been hired.

Example: If you were going to hire a candidate to represent your organization to outside constituents, then consider a breakfast meeting and a lunch meeting. Watch how they interact and treat the customer service staff while you are out. This is very reflective of how they may treat your constituents, clients, and associates. These are typically inexpensive meal opportunities to get a feel for another person.

You could also schedule a dinner meeting. Insist that they order first, as this may reveal how they will treat your wallet (expense forms, company credit card, etc.) if hired. If they are careless here, you may be heading in the direction of a high-maintenance employee. I have never been proven incorrect with this ... If they order the special and drink and dessert, enjoy the meal and never hire them – they will always have values in conflict with the health, wealth and vitality of long-term talent success – every time.

Evaluate the alignment and comfort each other has with one another from a diversity perspective for example? Education and additional talent development work initiatives may be needed to ensure success for all parties involved ...

The greater your understanding is of one another, the better you can select the best candidate for your organization, make them an offer, and begin the onboarding sequence and experience.

The ability to recognize great Human-Capital Talent that you can immediately leverage as an asset is not selfish, it's just good business. The candidate you are interviewing should be looking at you the same way. If they're not... run!

Here are some sobering analytics on human capital in the workplace.

A recent Gallup Poll of thousands of businesses surveyed revealed that:

1. **56 percent of** individuals in the workplace self-assessed as "disengaged in the workplace or complacent." In essence, what is the least I can do for the greatest compensation?

2. **15 percent** indicated that they are "actively disengaged or hostile" to their employer, colleagues and organization, routinely believing that business owners and leaders are biased against all employees and take advantage of them. Here is a great KPI for reflection to ensure that this is not an outgrowth of miss alignment in the DEI intentions.

3. **29 percent** are "actively engaged" in the workplace – here is where your pure human-capital talent is located.

Utilize all of the talent acquisition vetting processes that you can to determine the true color of the candidate that you are about to onboard. Remember, it can take a lifetime to create greatness and it can be imploded instantly with one wrong mis-hire.

Before you make the employment offer, consider requiring a few final steps. There are a host of outsourced professional firms that you can send a candidate to, for example, for drug screening, both as a final vetting step and as an outsourced employment process safety valve. You are creating a legal wall between you and the candidate. If they fail the drug test, you don't have to hire them. These same professional service firms can also perform a version of a *"Fit-For-Duty"* examination, as well, to ensure that your candidate can actually physically do the job. This vetting step, done by an outsourced third party, ensures that you don't hire an individual and set them up for talent failure. It will also protect your existing talent and organization away from mis-hiring an individual with deceitful intent, which can have a damaging impact on your organization.

You can, in many situations and with many layers of operating talent needs for your organization, partner with an outsourced Contract Labor firm that will vet and find ideal individuals to perform work that you need. This can serve as a pathway to full-time employment within your organization, yet for seasonal work needs or labor intense positions, this may also be a more economical and effective talent-management flow option.

Human-Capital Acquisition also requires evaluation of the quality of work/life balance, workplace environment and financials. Sometimes your talent management and retention issues may be set up for failure right here, before you ever onboard someone. Consider the overall compensation package for the talent you are seeking and willing to onboard and evaluate how that compensation package will need to possibly evolve over time to maintain and retain key talent for your organization. Be strategic and offensive in your posture, so you never find yourself in a defensive position to retain.

Just as there are a myriad of options to finding and vetting prospective candidates for consideration for your organization, there are also options to accelerate the quality of candidates you interview. There's a myriad of resources, industry analytics and online portals for assessing and job scoping a position for determination of fair market compensation. Know what you must invest in to get great talent and be ready to speak to this, if raised in the acquisition, interviewing, discussion phases.

You should also consider the multitude of social medial platforms today that talent organization's can access and provide you critical insight data in evaluating a prospective new addition to your organization. Likewise, you should review the social media footprint a person has and look back over the past year or so, to ensure that your *values, vision and culture* would be enhanced by a person you are considering being added to your team, and not be damaged by being added to your team. Remember the time tested adage, *"birds of a feather flock together"* and while it can be said *"guilt by association"* it can also be said *"success by association"* so do your homework early and build winning teams, and avoid HR trauma after-the-fact!

When you feel confident to add to your talent pool, ask yourself how you and others in the organization will connect with the next new addition to your team? Human Capital is great currency within an organization, but always recognize if you have to manage egos all day long, is that an ROI you can live with?

Talent Acquisition is a critical step in the talent process.

Remember, the overall employee experience is shaped and determined by how you (individually and organizationally) manage your side of each of the ACHIEVEMENT life cycle phases and what the individual employee receives, sees, observes, and internalizes as their EXPERIENCE along the way. Every touchpoint from the organization, whether intentional or unintentional, whether overt or not, still shapes the experience an individual has within the work environment.

As you undertake this important Third phase of the ACHIEVE-MENT life cycle, always stay focused on how this applies to the

TALENT in a multitude of applications. For an organization, it demands the understanding of each application and how they actually must align as one for ultimate ROI. Identify at each of the following five TALENT considerations, what do you expect the new talent to do, i.e., what are the TDRs. This must be done first because it leads into the next crucial step: what KSAs are required to perform the role (TDR) you plan to put them in:

1. TALENT management of the INDIVIDUAL;

2. TALENT management of career PATHWAYS;

3. TALENT management of critical essential POSITION pathways;

4. TALENT management of secondary support POSITION pathways; and

5. TALENT management of the ORGANIZATION.

Understanding the life cycle of TALENTification is critical and we hope this book helps synthesize what we know about human capital and provides a simplified approach for individuals and organizations to move beyond the carousel of the past.

The understanding of the acquisition, onboarding, developmental and exit interview process provides never-ending data to design and implement a talent-management process that will allow any organization to recognize and leverage their greatest competitive asset in the new world economy – HUMAN CAPITAL!

Chapter Four

Integrate DEI & On-Boarding Talent

Integrating Onboarding – Getting new hires to the organization in a quick, efficient and robust way has shown to be one of the biggest factors in attitude formation by these new hires. This is much more than pointing people to a vast amount of information posted on the organization's website; it is essential that there is a personal, human touch to onboarding and integrating people into the organization and into their new role. The speed with which people become knowledgeable and effective in their role is accelerated by the assimilation. The popularity of books like _The First 90 Days_ or _Right From The Start_ are a testament to this.

Onboarding talent should also be a reflection of the DEI goals of the organization. Here is where you may want to pause and reflect on the uniqueness of the individual and tailor that onboarding experience for the first 30-60-90-120-days from both an HR process needs and the supervising manager area as well. Provide a DEI-Sponsor or Advocate to serve as a secondary talent resource to ensure the new hire feels a sense of belonging, inclusion and is valued.

All next steps aligned with previous KPIs: *30-, 60-, 90-, 120-day minimum formal structured integration and check-up checkpoints; Technician v. Operational Effectiveness milestones; Ensuring new Talent blend, support and grow Business Plans, Mission Statements and Values; Talent life cycle process identified and initiated by Position, Tenure, Individual Aspirations, Organizational Needs, Compliance to Job Position Statements, Market Needs and Attrition Needs; Initial Professional Development Plans* **(PDP)** *and needs aligned with individual aspirations; Assigned a sponsor or mentor as secondary alignment resource; Artificial Intelligence* **(AI)** *is a player; Champions; Etc.*

This initial onboarding process must be owned by the human resource manager (and/or someone specifically on that team), the immediate hiring manager, and if these are different than the immediate employee's (or executive's) reporting manager, then all three as a minimum. Any specifically assigned sponsor/mentor/accountability partner should also be figured into the daily/weekly/monthly check-in opportunities, with specific KPIs as a road map along the 30-, 60-, 90-, 120-day minimum formal structured integration.

You may also want to explore building and staffing an Employee **Engagement Group (EEG)** or sometimes called an **Employee Resource Group (ERG)** made up of a cross section of demographics to ensure the health and stability of your human capital, labor force. This group can be empowered to advocate for the organization and identify employee needs to be advocated to the organizational leadership. This is an inclusive employee integration group to compliment the HR efforts and the Supervising Manager of a new hire or new promotable.

It's is difficult to be INCLUSIVE today and tomorrow, if all you want to discuss or litigate is yesterday's EXCLUSIVITY issues.

DEI is not just about the NUMBERS or Diversity of White versus Black ethnicity, or female versus male gender, etc. It is about being INCLUSIVE to allow people to be Authentic within an organization, that is in ALIGNEMENT with that organizations Values, Vision, Beliefs and Mission first!

The reality in most organizations is that new hires are brought into an organization with the best intentions of integrating them effectively into the organization and into their respective work teams, but the reality in most situations is opposite. Within hours or days of the new arrival, everyone gets busy with daily SOPs, life and unexpected issues. The next things missed are the scheduled regular check-in or update touchpoints, and then it is a fast six months down the road when everyone realizes the new hire is off trajectory or derailing. They have been left to fend for themselves and learn for themselves.

The effective Integration Onboarding of a new hire should be a very intentional process. If you have the luxury of a Chief Leadership Officer otherwise your Learning & Development Team, they need to be aligned and collaborate to ensure a seamless transition from new ire onboarding KPIs into sustained life success internally to the organization and their strategic business unit. There should transition any new hire or internal transfer promotion individual into their echo system once the initial on-boarding has taken place.

Paradigms of human resource must evolve as well, among individuals in the organization and within management, leadership, executive ranks and the Board levels. For example, it used to be about **ASSIMILATION**, this is very old school; you must abandon all that is you and adopt all that is us business paradigm. Then we were about **DIFFERENTIATION**, which really meant exclusion at the end of the conversation. To leverage human capital and the valuable diversity around you, it really is about **INTEGRATION** and how we can leverage each other for greatness.

Here is another opportunity to shine organizationally. Have a Champion or Advocate that represents your best DEI expectations to embrace this individual as an additional alignment partner to flow them through your process and organization. Ensure the are included and feel welcomed, appreciated and utilized.

You need to plan this out as if you were designing a very detailed flight plan from Earth past the Sun to a neighboring Planet, any miscalculation ends in death – be that emphatic about your approach and you will create an intentional environment and culture of excellence in all that you do!

Before you consider viewing this interaction from the organization's perspective outward to each new and existing member of your organization, make sure that you have clarity of their expectations inward towards you (defer to the Player Capability Index modeling presented earlier, here is where it once again will come to life):

1. What are the aspirations, goals (immediate, intermediate and long-term) of the individual?
2. What are the individual's expectations of the organization with regard to themselves?
3. What are the individual's expectations of the leadership with regard to themselves?
4. What are the individual's expectations of the business unit that they are being integrated into?
5. What are the expectations of the individual, if any, of their coworkers with regard to themselves?

These insights are critical to ensuring that you onboard effectively, align and integrate effectively, and will save you tremendous challenges in the future by keeping great talent. It is the failure of talent leadership to know these insights from before day one that compounds and creates internal talent development and retention issues.

In understanding differences and thus DEI initiatives and best practice, we live in a world of derailers to successful talent management. One of those is through the Micro Aggressions that define all of us. Those ways we have been raised, influenced, conditioned, educated and corrected throughout our lives as to how to think, feel and operate. These Micro Aggressions can appear in many ways:

- Verbal, in how we talk or don't talk and what is said or implied.
- Environments
- Behaviors
- Policies
- Actions

These can all cause someone to feel unwelcomed or discriminated against.

Some remedies that all of us can consider to reduce and eliminate Micro Aggressions, could be:

- Employ Diverse Teams and create advocacy groups like Employee Resource Groups (ERG) or Employee Engagement Groups (EEG)
- Training for everyone
- Identify the culture you want and ensure everyone understands this and is buying into this
- Sign Post what you are about everywhere
- Do regular risk assessments
- Offer bystander training
- If you are a leader be the catalyst

Considerations:

1. Human Resource Onboarding – The first stop for new hires on this onboarding sequence should be with HR for all of the official, legal, health, financial, contracting, employee handbook review, etc., documentations and necessary instruction on just how to operate within the new environment … Have a checklist to ensure day-one, week-one, month-one onboarding flows smoothly and creates an experience of acceptance and welcome of new talent; that all compliance actions are addressed; and the new hire is integrated to achieve maximum acceptance and minimal anxiety … Make sure to have designed, implemented and determined the accountability flow so as to not forget that

similar new hire check-in points at monthly intervals for the first year may bring enhanced ROI.

2. Key Stakeholders – Ensure new hires are introduced to all of the immediate key stakeholders with the ability to help them operate and perform in their assigned role. Take the mystique out of personnel and personalities and schedule time for them to shadow or have a one-on-one meet-and-greet with appropriate senior leaders and key stakeholders. This will enable them to get an official understanding of the totality of the organization and how all of the pieces of the business interface, flow and work.

3. Job Shadowing – Depending upon the role the new hire will serve, let them rotate around the business unit the role functions within shadowing your superstars in each role or function, so they are acclimated to peak performance in each area.

4. Immediate Manager – The immediate manager needs to onboard the new hire to their specific TDR and ensure they know how to hit the ground running. As determined prior to hiring them, the immediate manager can also outline the developmental sequence for KSAs, as required to perform the role; have a checklist to ensure day-one, week-one, month-one onboarding flows smoothly and creates an experience of acceptance and welcome of new talent; that all "compliance" actions are addressed; and the new hire is integrated to achieve maximum acceptance and minimal anxiety.

5. Aspirations – Ensure as you map out these considerations onto a calendar system that their aspirations, your aspirations for them as the immediate manager, and the organizations aspirations for both of you and the team are in alignment and being met.

6. Mentor/Sponsor/Advocate/Champion – Create a lineup of your best talent to serve as mentors for new talent onboarding, integration and effectiveness. Mentors should not be supervisors of the new employee; but other proven, great stewards of your organization that can be shepherds of new talent to ensure they are understanding the dynamics of the organization, their job responsibilities and to help with any questions that may come up. The Mentor can be a in a direct line area to them or one removed. They ensure that the new talent is integrating into the organization and connecting with others as efficiently as possible.

7. Job Rotation – In some organizations it may serve, as both an awareness and educational understanding fulfillment, to rotate new hires early on in their onboarding process, throughout their specific work area, team or group. This also allows a new colleague to very quickly get exposure to all members of the team and at a cursory level the work flow dynamics. This will help them gain a better understanding of what they do by understanding some of the roles before and after their own.

8. Employee Resource Group or Employee Engagement Group is another powerful means to on-boarding and in-boarding new talent to ensure they are welcomed, comfortable, feel as sense of bellowing and championed into the organization and into their specific business unit. This group should in itself be a diverse cohesive aligned group of professionals with the organizations Value system serving as its GPS or North Star as some may call it. This group of selected or volunteers serve as a force multiplier for the human resource team to ensure success of every

individual and as a sounding board for ideas, news ides and potential concerns to be presented, back-and-forth.

9. DEI(A) Training – Ensure educational motivational experiential
training programs facilitated by inhouse Subject-Matter-Experts and outside talent to provide everyone with best in time
understanding of DEI(A) and the ACHIEVEMENT Process.
Look at live instruction, virtual reinforcement, coaching, access
to educational resources.

**If you really want to accelerate a new hire into your organization
and inspire them to greatness, consider these additional strategies:**

10. Senior Leader Shadowing – Allow them to spend a day or two
with the senior leaders, executives or the owner and glean from
them what right looks like.

11. Organization, Plant, or Enterprise Tour – As appropriate, make
sure that new talent has an opportunity early on to get exposure
to the entire operation, so as to better understand the enterprise
and what they do within it. This will also expose them to your
other rockstar talent and evaluate from their own lens the global
opportunities with the organization. This also plants seeds of
awareness in their head as to ways they can serve the entire business, including referring outside talent to the organization!

12. Team Scene - Create a social event for new hires, new transfers
or interns to meet and assimilate efficiently with peers and leaders alike. Ideas include shared Profile exchanges (resume, bios,
LinkedIn Connection, etc. for advanced insights of one another), power breakfasts, lunch exchanges, etc., to introduce and
acclimate to one another.

As you integrate them initially onto the team, make sure you use existing instruments (you don't need to be constantly reinventing the wheel) as a means to ensure maximum integration and efficiencies. Defer to their Performance assessment or Coaching documentation. While your organization may officially use these instruments on an Annual, Semi-Annual or Quarterly basis, you can use these as conversational instruments on a weekly wrap-up, debrief, review opportunities in a one-one-one setting or as a team peer-to-peer coaching interaction.

Make sure that the expectation milestones for becoming acclimated into the organization are being measured, monitored and met. Make sure that the milestones for work product quality and quantity are being measured, monitored and met. Make sure social goals for integrating with the team, as appropriate, are being measured, monitored and met.

Here is where a great 30-, 60-, 90-day structured discussion should take place. Consider at each of these three distinct times, the talent conversation between the new hire and their Hiring Manager or Reporting Manager:

1. *Job Description* – Discuss line-by-line how they are performing each line item at that date point. Discuss questions that need to be addressed. Identify level of effectiveness that is being executed at that point and if there is additional learning or resources needed.

2. *Performance Review* – In an informal manner, discuss line-by-line how they will be measured officially at organizationally designated times during their Performance review, which is aligned

to the Job Description they were hired to perform. Discuss questions that need to be addressed. Identify level of effectiveness that is being executed at that point and if there is additional learning or resources needed.

3. *Employee Handbook* – Another great opportunity, as you are onboarding new talent to ensure that they are on the correct and desired performance trajectory from day one is at these 30-, 60-, 90-day reviews. Just revisit and review key conduct expectations in this handbook with them.

4. *Personal Expectations* – Discuss or revisit previous onboarding discussions (even better if documented) around their expectations of: (A) The position or role they are executing, and whether it is fulfilling all expectations and whether it is in alignment with their personal/professional goals and aspirations; (B) The organization, and whether it is fulfilling all expectations and whether it is in alignment with their personal/professional goals and aspirations; (C) The immediate managing manager they are working with or for, and whether that person is fulfilling all expectations and whether they are in alignment with their personal/professional goals and aspirations?

Make sure that the onboarding Professional Development Plans (**PDPs**) are designed with detailed developmental KPIs on both the technician side of their position and the professional development side in mind; that the new hire is not being overwhelmed; and that they are getting traction in their position. That allows you to start to disengage from them as they become an independent operating member of them team – management should be seen, but not always present.

From a human resourcing developmental track, every position should also have a formal and informal developmental plan that is tied in with human resources or the training and development enterprises within the organization. Make sure that the new hire, as for every employee, has a clear pathway of KSA professional development mapped out to engage and enrich them from day one and throughout their life span within the organization and the talent life cycle.

Another means of accelerating peer acceptance is the utilization of social-style or personality-style indexing instruments. There is a wide array of options in the marketplace. To generate the maximum ROI from these assessments, make sure you coach the new hire on the findings and what they mean to them for better interactions, communications, and engagement with others. Discuss not only the findings and how they can better manage themselves and grow themselves more effectively, make sure the instruments provide cross analysis as to how the new hire and others will best interact with one another.

Identify all of the breakpoints to successful Integration Onboarding of a new hire (whether that is a new person to your organization or an internal transfer), and make sure you have people and systems in place to guard against obvious areas that cause frustrations, discouragement, disengagement, company or mental checkout by the new person. Think of the last new hire you had to a team, organization or project, and recall any breakpoints or gaps that were missed entering the experience, yet developed, and either did or could have lead to an implosion and fix them. Think of this through administrative optics: what resources does one need to even function; if any of those are missing, you have set the new hire up for frustrations and possibly even failure just as they are getting started.

Make sure that the integration process addresses the talent needs of the new hire from an immediate, intermediate and long-term perspective. Further, see that the new hire is meeting the expectations of the managers (supervisory, hiring, human resources, etc.), so that everyone is in alignment with organization expectations and need requirements.

Whether you are in a leadership capacity, business ownership or employee, there should be a fiercely objective set of analytics or a human resources dashboard that reveals where any individual lies in regard to talent capacity (as both a technician in their job role and functionality, as well as overall professional acumen and development) that clearly indicates the next talent growth initiative expectations for measurement. Ultimate talent development, integration and growth should be about elevating every individual to be as agile, nimble, flexible, and proactive as characteristics of the Talent Development pipeline in producing internal human capital 24/7.

As discussed before and throughout this book, the Onboarding and integration of a new hire or new transfer is critical to the ACHIEVE-MENT process. One powerful benchmark for individuals, peers and leadership is to ensure *compliance to Job Position statements*. Make sure these are relevant and always in a state of fluidity, meaning that what one expects and measures is accurate throughout and current. Regular check-up of these documents can be done by management and HR by asking the superstar in any Position if the document is current and accurate; allow for real-time feedback. As we will discuss in later aspects of this ACHIEVEMENT process, there should be a direct correlation at every level of your human-capital chain: between the Job/Role Expectations/Statements and the Performance Assessment or Reviews utilized at each level.

Remember, the overall employee experience is shaped and determined by how you (individually and organizationally) manage your side of each of the ACHIEVEMENT life cycle phases and what the individual employee receives, sees, observes, and internalizes as their EXPERIENCE along the way. Every touchpoint from the organization, whether intentional or unintentional, whether overt or not, still shapes the experience an individual has within the work environment.

AI influence and impact upon integrating, engaging, and effective talent inclusion will be critical for dynamic organizations. With this will be the ever-emerging technology platforms to aid human resources in this endeavor. While AI can be a major force multiplier, there will be no replacement for the human common-sense meter. Analytics and the optics it provides, are always database driven – good data analytics in, good analytics out; bad analytics in and misleading data out!

In considering any AI system, it should be a tool or resource that embodies the organization's Values, Vision and Mission Statement and allows for it to better address the inclusion, culture and business needs in respect to talent development and talent management of both the present and long-term needs for the organization. TALENTification is about everything one does and that an organization does to be relevant and no AI approach should simply serve as an AI system for a scorecard to be created that an organization is checking the box of labor relation and governmental diversity balances at the expense of the actual organizations health.

Ideally, AI should accelerate the talent KSA mapping of the individual, with the present TDR Job Descriptions, in alignment with aspirations of both the employee/individual and their hiring-manager and supervising-manager. AI should be able to map this against organizational needs, market expectations and succession life cycles.

A key aspect of TALENTification is the responsibility of every supervising manager primarily, and hiring manager secondarily, to be cognizant of what each person on their team does, what their growth goals are, what their growth potential is within that business unit or within the organization overall. Talent gaps, lacks and losses should be ata minimum if the ACHIEVEMENT process is at work. Learning of an impending employee departure because of employment growth opportunities with another employer, whether it is because the employee did not see themselves within your organization or because you failed to articulate your strategic plans for them, is a failure of the TALENTification succession process.

Individuals, likewise, should be aware of the TALENTification process, as well, and should feel comfortable communicating with their supervising manager, hiring manager and senior leaders about the goals/aspirations they have and whether they feel those are being met.

Business/C-Suite leaders at their respective levels must architect out their immediate, intermediate and long-term talent needs, growth migration patterns of personnel and the ongoing professional development needs in order for their business enterprise to survive and thrive – from both the technician skills/aptitudes requirements and professional KSAs -- to perform the TDR expected.

Here is an example of what this on-boarding sequence might look like. This is a model crafted with one of our private sector business clients and their HR Team:

Onboarding: Best Practices

The Four "C's" of Onboarding	
Compliance:	Complete required government / organizational documents – policies and procedures
Clarification:	Ensure that the new Co-worker understands their role and expectations - their manager and the organization
Culture:	Assimilate new Co-worker into organizational norms – both formal and informal
Connection:	Establish interpersonal relationships and information networks for the new Co-worker to be successful

Optimize Results	Clarify Objectives	Clarify Delivery Expectations
Avoid Derailment	Provide Support	Expedite Understanding
Facilitate Integration	Team Operation	Establish Structure

The degree of culture disruption, productivity disruption and profitability disruption that an organization takes annually due to these failures is massive and on a global basis. Architect out individual player aspirations for positional efficiency, productivity, profitability and development as it relates to the individual ... align this with succession needs.

As you work through your on-boarding sequence that involves both the new talent to your organization, and involves all appropriate talent horizontally and vertically to that new talent, consider the implications and ramifications in four core areas as well:

1. Compliance
2. Clarification
3. Culture
4. Connection

An innovative way to enhance the onboarding and integration phases of new talent, while re-engaging existing talent, is to have a CHAMPION (*to be their Advocate, Sponsor, Go-to-Person, aside from their hiring manager and supervising manager*) in place and assigned to each new hire. Think of the CHAMPION as an individual who best embodies all that your organization strives to be, and make them a conduit between the new hire or new transfer and that team. A conduit and go-to person, aside from management, leadership and any official Mentor (that we will address in later Chapters), who will ensure the wellbeing of the new talent, whom the organization has already made a massive investment into finding, onboarding and now successfully integrating into both the organization and the specific work group.

Integrating and On-Boarding all talent into your organization, quick-check list considerations:

- Partner new hires with a Sponsor/Advocate
- Assign a Mentor
- Ensure Employee Resource Groups welcome new hires
- Establish 30-60-90-day performance calibration discussions with supervising manager
- Establish 30-60-90-day performance calibration discussions with hiring manager
- Identify new hires Knowledge, Skills, Abilities and ensure they are aligned into new role Tasks, Duties, Responsibilities

- Have a Values alignment check-up at 30-60-90-days

As you undertake this important Fourth phase of the ACHIEVE-MENT life cycle, always stay focused on how this applies to the TALENT in a multiple of applications. For an organization, it demands the understanding of each application and how they actually must align as one for ultimate ROI. Identify at each of the following five TALENT considerations, what do you expect the new talent to do, i.e., what are the TDRs. This must be done first because it leads into the next crucial step: what KSAs are required to perform the role (TDR) you plan to put them in:

1. TALENT management of the INDIVIDUAL;
2. TALENT management of career PATHWAYS;
3. TALENT management of critical essential POSITION pathways;
4. TALENT management of secondary support POSITION pathways; and
5. TALENT management of the ORGANIZATION.

Understanding the life cycle of TALENTification is critical and we hope this book helps synthesize what we know about human capital and provides a simplified approach for individuals and organizations to move beyond the carousel of the past.

The understanding of the acquisition, onboarding, developmental and exit interview process provides never-ending data to design and implement a talent-management process that will allow any organization to recognize and leverage their greatest competitive asset in the new world economy – HUMAN CAPITAL!

Chapter Five

Engage, Activate & Socialization Of DEI(A)

Engage, Activate & Socialize – All next steps aligned with previous KPIs: *Acceptance, Participation, Comfort, Sense of Belonging; Introducing and Advocating & Sponsoring New Talent into Organization and to Core Personalities; Talent life cycle by Position, Tenure, Individual Aspirations, Organizational Needs, Market Needs and Attrition Needs; Transfer of Learning & Creating the Learning Mindset Virally; Mentoring; Standard-of-Conduct Policies; Engaging the TALENTification Terrorist; ERG participation, Etc.*

Here is where talent decides to stay and contribute (engaged, inclusive), stay and go through the motions (complacent) or leave. Along with great managerial-leadership engagement and on-going coaching, you may want to explore other strategies, processes and programs that creates inclusion and provides pathways for equity in performance and opportunities. Create an Employee Resource Group (ERG), Employee Engagement Groups (EEG) or Diversity Network Groups to serve as talent advocates and diversity champions. Have a performance review check-ins or electronic assessments to gather on-going feedback.

Create DEI specific assessments for feedback by all employees and not just new hires in the onboarding processes or in-boarding of internal talent that moves or is promoted with, that seeks just feedback on Diversity, Equity and Inclusion factors you want to track or need to track.

Explore, develop and implement employee driven peer-to-peer recognition and achievement programs to further serve organically bottom-up behaviors you seek, along with top-down managerial-leadership same programs.

Career pathways and journey experiences should be considered for all employees here and especially as you reflect on the Diversity spreadsheet exercise in the ACHIEVEMENT Model **Awareness of DEI TALENT Life Cycle** step and the Human Capital Talent Outlook Report. Consider programs like Emerging Talent, Next-Gen, Emerging Leaders, or affinity development tracks like 20-under-20 or 30-under-30 talent programs or Emerging Women in Business/Leadership or Diversity Accelerators (there is no good way to name some of these initiatives) … The objective is to provide an accelerated development pathway for previously underrepresented groups that your organization can benefit from including.

Engage, Activate & Socialize – *All next steps aligned with previous KPIs - Acceptance, Participation, Comfort, Sense of Belonging; Introducing and Advocating & Sponsoring New Talent into Organization and to Core Personalities; Talent life cycle by Position, Tenure, Individual Aspirations, Organizational Needs, Market Needs and Attrition Needs; Transfer of Learning & Creating the Learning Mindset Virally; Mentoring; Standard-of-Conduct Policies; Engaging the TALENTification Terrorist; Etc.*

More than Maslow's Hierarchy of Needs is at play at this talent level. The ability of an organization to capture the heart, mind, soul and energy of new talent on day one is critical every day in the talent life cycle. While this may be a great afterthought human resourcing area, it is almost always at the root of every lost soul in an organization. How you embrace a new hire is in direct correlation to how you embrace one another within an organization. So, ask yourself as leaders or key stakeholders to the human-capital talent process, would you go out to breakfast or lunch with your colleagues? If you have a child, would you leave them in the care of your colleague? Interesting questions …

Evaluate from day one how you go about introducing a new member to the organization and team. Be cognizant of the diversity realities of both the organization and the individual, you may need to adjust, adopt and even create the engagement touchpoints throughout the ACHIEVEMENT™ Process to be sensitive to diversity protocols to ensure inclusion integration success. Here is a great place to engage an DEI Employe Engagement Group or Team for feedback and participation.

This will set the stage for how that person will grow and feel accepted. Think of this just like K-12 education.

1. We go to elementary school to learn and understand the basics and fundamentals needed to survive and then thrive – so, too, should the early onboarding days be for a new hire. Make sure you support them, resource them, mentor or champion them for early foundational days of getting stable within the organization for success. Make sure that you have Systems in play to integrate new hires to the organization, just as having everything in play for existing talent who is transferred or promoted. Along with the talent-management staff, hiring or managing supervisor, also have a go-to person to ensure that they are being integrated effectively and that there are no assumptions being made on an individual basis.

2. Once those basics are understood or determined mastered, then it is off to secondary level (high school), where the concentration, now, is on application of what one knows in this environment as applicable to their role or job function. From a talent management perspective, this is where you have continual opportunities for more education, experience and interactions with others that allow you to further integrate individuals to the team, and where you start to see greater levels of activated energy, insights, collaboration and ownership take place. This is where you start to see Subject-Matter Experts reveal themselves and where you can start to recognize the hidden talent existing within your organization.

A Simple, yet meaningful, way to engage talent is to always be open to talent involvement. A new set of eyes and ears can sometimes bring you great insights as to how to improve and accelerate success. Consider with everyone in your organization regularly:

1. Acceleration Opportunities – Create an environment wherein individuals can brainstorm, either one-on-one or in group situations, ways to improve any System, Process, Procedure and Deliverable you have.

2. Improvement Teams – Whereby you create a collaboration opportunity for individuals cross horizontal and vertical work lines come together at the beginning, midway or conclusion of endeavors to evaluate what worked and did not work and ways to improve the next undertaking.

3. Employee Resource Groups (ERG) or Employee Engagement Groups/teams (EEG) or Diversity Network Group (DNG) – It does not really matter what you call it, the intent here is to have a group of organic volunteered labor that can come together regularly to serve … Each said group could ideally have as an auditing sponsor or advocate a senior leader in the organization.

As an emotional support, one-on-one collective when needed, comprised as a safe space for people to ask, share, learn and deal with critical issues, to create a sense of belonging, it could be driven by a weekly topic that bring people together and builds towards greater unity and alignment. This group could then push KPIs upward to management and leadership, they can feed legitimate business issues into the echo system for discussion well in advance of issues become crises point. This group can be an innovation incubator from their diverse talents and seeing the organization through their unique lens. In seeing DEI from their frontline lens, they can be early influencers for success and addressing potentially toxic KPIs. Here is another great opportunity for the considerations around accessibility to be consciously addressed. They can thus serve as a resource to one another and to each other for a great sense of culture and value driven organization.

4. New Hire Lens – Create a pathway opportunity for new hires to really ask the "WHY" questions to everything that you do and invite candid feedback at any point for insights on how they see you being: Better, more Efficient or Faster, Different than everyone else in the market, and/or more Cost Effective in what you do.

5. Resume/Job Description Challenge – Another way to integrate, activate and encourage social interaction with new hires and existing talent is to identify from their resume where their power talent lies and align that to specific job duty needs. Then elevate them to situationally lead discussions, meetings, or tasks that play to their bench strength.

6. Job Rotation – Keeping the new hire's energy and enthusiasm high can also be maintained by a regular opportunity to rotate through positions connected to their actual work-product position. It may serve as both an awareness and educational understanding fulfillment to rotate employees, in general and at any tenure capacity within an organization, to gain a better real-time understanding of what they do by understanding some of the job roles around them within an organization. This may also organically generate interest in your talent pool for other opportunities horizontally and vertically within your organization that may not have otherwise recognized!

7. Alignment of Aspirations – To fully Engage, Activate and Socialize new hires and existing members of an organization in a meaningful manner, leadership (both the Hiring Manager and Supervising Manager [if different]) must know individuals' sequential aspirations within the organization and on their career pathway, to ensure that one is being engaged in alignment to their vision and expectations.

8. Stretch Goals – Always be assessing the ability, desire and capacity of an individual to explore what they have deeper within themselves and aligning that with stretch opportunities, experiences, challenges that will grow them, while demonstrating to management, leadership, colleagues and themselves where their potential lies.

By having clear lines of progression, pathways for each position and the deliverables expected from a person in a position, you will also see engaged energy from individuals. Talent leaders must understand and know that some people see career progression as the ability to remain in their present position and continue to grow, achieve and contribute from that level – there is nothing negative to be read into this. Others see career progression as a continued journey within an organization – and that must be recognized and addressed, as well.

Research also indicates that organizations that create and operate Mentoring programs see a greater retention rate of talent at every involved level (more on Mentoring styles and application concepts in Chapter Seven and Table 7.2 Five Different Mentor Styles/Types: The Mentor Life Cycle). So from the reality of your business enterprise, consider ways to formally and informally pair up individuals so they can support one another, learn from one another, and guide one another for energized talent development.

Socialization can be achieved, as you can see, as a byproduct of many undertakings within an organization. Most people do like to participate and be a part of an organization where there is some degree of fun, enthusiasm, celebration, comradery and mutual support. The list of ways to generate re-energizing social opportunities are endless, and no matter what the size of your organization is, you can engage in these types of activities.

1. Monthly Celebrations – Of business accomplishments, production achievements, new hire onboarding, employee anniversary dates, organization milestones, etc.

2. Monthly Calendar Dates – Remember back to elementary school, every month had a holiday date worth celebrating and we did so back in the day. One major residual benefit was it gave every student the opportunity to stop and think about everyone else and join in on the celebrations. All of this aside from our normal work day activities; we stopped for a minute and just socialized.

3. Peer to Peer Recognition – Create an recognition program driven by peers catching others in actions of greatness, so it can be showcased, called out and lifted up to reinforce the organization goals, projects, programs, needs and even wrapped around DEI. Allow for tangible acknowledgements driven by awards, points, bonuses, etc.

4. New Hire & Retirement Celebrations – Understanding the talent ACHIEVEMENT life cycle could not be better articulated than when we celebrate a member of our organization who has

served us well and is retiring. We reflect back upon their career and talent contributions and we do so in a celebratory manner that allows for socialization. This, too, should be how we start each talent acquisition to an organization: with a celebration and welcome to the team, to celebrate their resume as additional talent to the team for everyone's awareness.

5. Communication – The larger the organization is, the more challenging it may be to do these ideas; but you can ensure celebration by ensuring you regularly communicate these same KPIs via your internal message boards, website, social media platforms, etc. The more everyone knows, the more connected everyone is, and the greater level of socialization can be among everyone!

6. State of the Organization – As done with many organizations, on a regular basis (monthly perhaps) the senior leadership brings everyone together for a socialization opportunity (Town hall sort of breakfast, coffee, luncheon) to share the state of the state with everyone. The power of this is that leadership is in control of the official messaging to everyone and it pulls everyone in from every facet of the business to understand where the organization is today and how everyone plays a role in the good, the bad, and the ugly, as they say. Opportunities for success can be shared and the call for talent ideas can be hailed.

7. Team/Department/Organization Outreach – The opportunity for talent to self-organize into groups for off-the-clock athletic undertakings, community volunteer endeavors, or special event activities that are in alignment with your Organizations Employee handbook and Values is another powerful way for

integrating, emerging, and activating talent and providing socialization opportunities.

8. Mentoring – As discussed in other areas of this book, creating a
   structured mentoring program to onboard or inboard talent and
   pair them up whereas the mentor and mentee can learn from
   one another and growth the organization stronger, always a valuable undertaking.

9. Sponsor – Different than a mentor, the Sponsor is a great pairing
   at level three (H) and four (I) of the ACHIEVEMENT Process
   model, and throughout the life cycle of a person in your organization. The Sponsor is another go to contact for an employee
   should they have questions they are unsure where to be directed
   and the sponsor can be a great welfare check-in to make sure
   everyone is always heathy.

What is found, is that in organizations whereby more people feel
interconnected with one another than not, those teams excel greater,
accomplish more, and in tough times, pull together more freely,
willingly and substantially.

On a deeper talent-engagement level, to integrate new talent to the
organization and integrate existing talent that one may need to re-
engage and activate, here are further considerations:

1. Wins – Human-Capital psychology loves to achieve and be successful at what they do, so the faster that organizations can create pathways for individuals to contribute and experience wins,
   the more individuals will want to win. Winning is a natural psychological high and stimulates talent to want to achieve more
   and more often!

2. Pathway Migration – Make sure individuals and leadership understand that the consistent achievement at a proficient level by talent, sets in motion typically an expectation of promotion, in opportunities, title, rank, etc. within an organization. This becomes a sort of expressed commitment between the organization and the talent and must be adhered to. When it is not, this can become a major catalyst for exiting talent within an organization.

3. Educational Development – Leverage the educational growth of everyone within your organization and have them share with others freely. Have a forum by which, when you invest in the development of current talent, they can share with others – have a brown bag lunch when someone comes back from a new training, off-site experience, sabbatical, or off-site traveling and share. Turn everyone on your team into situational Subject-Matter Experts via an online webinar or open form video conference. Save best-practice learning into an archived vault for internal colleague access, etc.

4. Meaningful KPI Dates – To ensure active minds and bodies in the workplace, make sure that you have regular performance check-in points on the calendar related to specific job responsibility accomplishments. Benchmark these into performance review conversations and against career pathway expectations each person may have. Even more importantly is to ensure that each person is progressing, developing and achieving as the organization needs them to for talent development progression. The succession development, management and migration of individuals within an organization is a foremost obligation of the talent leadership within an organization.

It is not the sole responsibility of the organization or leaders to get individuals involved or to activate their engagement or to ensure that everyone socializes and likes one another. However, it is the responsibility of the organization and leadership, especially those in the talent management pipeline, to create opportunities and pathways for socialization to occur!

Another means by which an organization can calibrate the minds, souls and hearts of its members is to have a living document crafted by the key stakeholders that details out what is and is not acceptable behavior and actions on the job and off, as it pertains to employment and associations with your organization – these are referred to as Standard-of-Conduct Policies. How you engage one another within your organization, will reveal a lot about how your people engage others within their communities. View your Standard-of-Conduct Policies as the blueprint for what is and is not acceptable in respect to everything you would want outsiders to brag most about in your organization. It makes it clear for everyone, at every level, at any time, what is acceptable, legal, ethical and moral as good citizens of your organization.

A key aspect of TALENTification is the responsibility of every supervising manager primarily, and hiring manager secondarily, to be cognizant of what each person on their team does, what their growth goals are, and that it is transparent where you see people growing into within that business unit or within the organization overall. Talent gaps, lacks and losses should be at a minimum if the ACHIEVEMENT process is at work – DEI should not be a stand-alone topic of discussion, it is just good sound business and it is what is done. Learning of an impending employee departure to pursue employment growth opportunities with another employer -- because an employee did not see themselves within your organization or because you failed to articulate your strategic plans, which included them -- is a failure of the TALENTification succession process.

Individuals, likewise, should be aware of the TALENTification process, as well, and be comfortable communicating with their supervising manager, hiring manager and senior leaders about the goals/aspirations they have and whether they feel those are being met.

Business/C-Suite leaders at their respective levels must architect out their immediate, intermediate and long-term talent needs, growth migration patterns of personnel and the ongoing professional development needs for their business enterprise to survive and thrive – including both the technician skills/aptitudes requirements and the professional KSAs to perform the TDR expected.

The degree of culture disruption, productivity disruption and profitability hits an organization takes due to these failures is massive on an annual and global basis. Architect out individual player aspirations for positional efficiency, productivity, profitability and development as it relates to the individual ... align this with succession needs.

If your organization and business units really want to engage and activate the mental and physical abilities of its human capital, then everyone should be, within reason, expected to stand up and participate. Organizations across the globe are facing a major threat to their survival and a direct impediment to an organization's ability to accelerate and thrive, and that is the equation of SUSTAINABIL-ITY!

By sustainability, we are talking in this context about the human capital within your organization and how you keep the best and eliminate the rest.

The topic of sustainability has, for decades, been owned by the linear-thinking and linearly charged positions – analytics, finance, accounting, engineering, operations, administration, etc. Sustainability is a 360-degree conversation and application – each business unit, including the entire C-Suite, has an ownership stake in understanding and implementing sustainability strategies and behaviors. Sustainability is a universal issue and is more far-reaching and impactful on an organization and the human capital they represent, than how most would entertain the concept of sustainability.

Far too often what we see in our marketplace is a survivor mentality, which serves as a cancer to sustainability. Engage your people and experience how to thrive!

The business annals are littered with business organizations and individuals that embraced survivor mentality and no longer exist. Conversely, the annals also boast many great organizations in the private sector and non-profit spaces that are thriving, sustainable best-in-class examples.

In 1971, the United States Junior Chamber of Commerce (aka US Jaycees) had more than one million members as a thriving, sustainable organization. By 2019, the US Jaycees are in survival mode and boast less than 30,000 members across the USA. They are knocking on death's doorstep of defeatism. Their Mission Statement from nearly 100 years ago is still 100 percent viable, but decades of flawed execution has become its GPS to derailment.

In the past decade, the United Methodist Church has lost more than one million members at their local-level leadership positions because of survivor mentality and not adjusting to a progressive, forward-focused thriving sustainability mindset.

The concept of sustainability has been bastardized in business conversation of late as applying only when discussing topics such as "green and/or conservation" or "ecological and/or alternative energy" or "global warming" applications. This is a gross misrepresentation of the concept. In that context, sustainability is a mere marketing gambit to attract people to false emotionally charged narratives and business endeavors that would otherwise not be profitable or relevant – it makes people feel good all over, in those cases, to say they are engaged in sustainable practices. Understanding TALENTification and the ACHIEVEMENT model allows an organization to become not only best in class and an employer of choice, it also elevates the discussion around sustainability to a new level and makes it a mandate for engaging and activating your human capital – at every level.

Sustainability in organizations is a universal and should be considered, benchmarked and applied in many ways. Here are a few non-traditional lenses, albeit not conclusive, to look through when considering the matter of "Sustainability."

1. *SUSTAINABILITY through Values=Visions=Mission Statement:* This is where thriving organizations live. These three variables serve as the GPS from which all other factors are borne. It

starts with a deep reflection on the organization's core key stakeholders' personal Values and how those evolve into the organization's Value System. Values drive the Vision of the individual and organization. These are typically transferred into a public pronouncement known as a Mission Statement. This is what every endeavor, deliverable, decision, and all human-capital moves should be aligned to for execution (meeting minimum business standards to stay viable, determining performance standards to attain a thriving state).

2. **SUSTAINABILITY through Viable Evolving Real-Time Deliverables:** Keeping people focused in a short-term world perspective, when the long-term matters is paramount for sustainability – on a level of being relevant in the immediate time frame and for the long term! To be sustainable, organizations must embrace a culture and attitude of agility to ensure what they engage in as a business, via business practices, deliverables, etc., serve a real and not manufactured false-narrative market need. The "this is what we have always done" thinking must be respectfully challenged at all times and with every incident. Conversely, just because an organization is executing action plans and deliverables, doesn't stipulate a need for change just for change if it does not serve a viable purpose that takes the organization to a thriving state.

Survival sustainability will be predicated upon the analytics of your present deliverables (as an organization or non-profit). Calculating those against the demographics you serve, what really is profitable, and what your organization should remain connected to and what should be spun-off to remain viable. Once this is done and monitoring systems and processes are in place for constant data feedback, then the organization's C-Suite owns the task of ensuring the viability of survival tomorrow by recognizing what the market will tolerate and need in the immediate, intermediate, and long-term future and determining ways to be market ready as those needs appear.

With a thriving sustainability mentality, organizations and their C-Suite (assisted by an engaged Board of Directors) will know and create the future so as to actually lead the market into thriving sustainability.

1. *SUSTAINABILITY through Trajectory Codes®* (TC): Blending involved participants and their personal/professional values, goals, aspirations, and needs (on immediate, intermediate and long-term time frames) is known as one's TC. These individual TCs must be determined if they are in alignment with the organization's TC (gains, buy-in, alignment, and thriving energies). When the two constituent trajectories align, then organizations operate from a baseline of sustainable trust and organizations will experience daily thriving realities and advances. The organization's TC must be supported by every business practice within that organization and by all human capital. Thriving organizations derail and fight daily to merely survive when these TCs are not aligned. Simple examples of how this takes place is demonstrated through personal pet agendas and egos that get in the way.

   Watch the YouTube video http://youtu.be/TsWrtgre29A and gain a better understanding of TC modeling. See also http://www.barnesandnoble.com/w/your-trajectory-code-jeffrey-magee/1120376074?ean=9781119043232&itm=1&usri=97811190 43232

2. ***SUSTAINABILITY through Human Capital:*** Misaligned TCs must be set aside if organizations are to truly attract best-in-class human capital and be able to execute best-in-class practices -- to, in fact, be sustainable. Organizations that go beyond merely survival mode have one guaranteed variable in play: they have the right human capital in the right place at the right time, and are endeavoring to cultivate a strong human-capital bench two to three levels inward or downward!

3. Human Capital involves a deep understanding of a wide cross section of diversity drivers. Understanding and applying generational diversity as an asset mentality; cultural imprinting on individuals and within the organization and the sub-entities within organizations; as well as how other factors of ethnicity, religion, life-style, social-economic drivers, etc. impact sustainability.

4. ***SUSTAINABILITY through E-Business and Traditional Business:*** Whether your organization is based or operates within the e-world (internet) or the traditional brick-and-mortar world, sustainability adheres to this same conversation. A critical change agent factor differentiator is that in the e-world one must be even more responsive and agile to factors that impact sustainability. This allows for proactive organizations in addressing immediate needs (Survival Sustainability endeavors) and allows a pathway for organizations and individuals to evolve forward (Thriving Sustainability endeavors). Having connectivity into valued constituents, both internally and externally, will provide clear TCs for any organization, in any situation, to ensure thriving sustainable actions, commitments, deliverables and energies.

5. ***SUSTAINABILITY through Economics:*** Ensuring cash flow management in times of survival will ensure sustainable thriving business practices. Understanding scalability dictates whether an organization can evolve into thriving states such as how AR (Accounts Receivable), AP (Accounts Payable),

6. Compensation and Benefits, Inventory Control, Shared Partnership Resources, Budgeting & Planning, Investment in all Capital areas, etc., are managed.

7. ***SUSTAINABILITY through Next Generation ... Evolve or Die:*** Another aspect of sustainability is applicable to practically everything you do. From the Boardroom to the C-Suite and from the frontline to the customer, have a forward-focused initiative always on what the next generation deliverables might and must be. From the programs and policies that foster thriving energies, to a 24/7 360-degree approach to developing your human capital forward/inward/upward, have the never-ending capacity to always be looking outward for what you can acquire, onboard, partner, and create as next-evolution realties.

8. ***SUSTAINABILITY through Engaged C-Suite Architecture:*** First, the Board should be aligned with your C-Suite in order for sustainability to be individually owned. The intent here is that as you establish the architecture layout of your C-Suite (i.e. CEO, CFO, COO, CIT, CLO ...), whether on paper for future implementation or in real-time and manned-up, you should have a dotted line from the CFO to a member of the Board who has had CFO experience, to be an accountability conduit of the CFO for and to the CEO and for the Board. This should be a mirrored dotted line concept for each person on your Board to ensure that you don't end up with multiple redundancies on the Board and

a C-Suite occupant with no advisory/accountability Board connection.

9. Second, each C-Suite position should be aligned to a Board member. They should be challenged to be evaluating and stress-testing present Sustainability factors within their respective enterprises for survival and then being pushed for action consideration for thriving sustainability opportunities – this takes engagement to a new level from the top down when implemented!

If you are thinking or actions within an organization are driven by stakeholders who fight for what is driving you to merely survive each day, then you will be limiting your possible reality. These people and this thinking are the factors that will challenge thriving sustainability. Sustainability relevance within your organization should no longer be one of unspoken shame!

Remember, the overall employee experience is shaped and determined by how you (individually and organizationally) manage your side of each of the ACHIEVEMENT life cycle phases and what the individual employee receives, sees, observes, and internalizes as their EXPERIENCE along the way. Every touchpoint from the organization, whether intentional or unintentional, whether overt or not, still shapes the experience an individual has within the work environment.

As discussed in previous chapters, it needs to be stated once again. Whether you are in a leadership capacity, business ownership or employee, there should be a fiercely objective set of analytics or a human resources dashboard that reveals where any individual lies in regard to talent capacity (as both a technician in their job role as well as overall professional acumen and development), that clearly indicates the next talent growth initiative expectations for measurement. Ultimate talent development, integration and growth should be about elevating every individual to be as agile, nimble, flexible, and proactive as the Talent Development pipeline in producing internal human capital 24/7.

A Special Note:

A special note on Individuals engaged in derailing the TALENTification ACHIEVEMENT process *(whom I have identified as and labeled as the "Terrorists" of civility, success and innovation among my writings, trainings and coaching for decades).*

For TALENTification processes and modeling to thrive, it is critical that the mad, sad, bad, entitlement oriented, and caustic employee be engaged. They are a cancer to the survival of your organization/society and a derailer to any DEI philosophy at the micro level that they operate within. And, left unchecked, they "kill" the ability for others to thrive and the ability of any business unit and the organization overall to succeed in their mission. An entire discussion can be held here of the devastating impact of one unchecked "Terrorist" in an organization.

Just as anyone hiding behind the banner of DEI and not contributing or holding unrealistic expectation is disingenuous to the true nature of what DEI is striving for – opportunity for all.

Communication and listening are critical in any business interaction and especially in areas where people may be expected to engage in new and forward focused ways. DEI(A) is not about using intersection language in an disingenuous manner to address one topic, while consciously creating a divisive bias. Or addressing one segmentation of human capital at the expense of another.

Again, here is another great opportunity to create, have and or engage your Employee Engagement Groups aka Employee Resource Group (ERG) that may be champions and advocates for DEI, along with a host of other business success initiatives.

Many of the leading talent development training firms of the past three decades have offered situational training courses and discussions to address this element, that I have designed. We provide a powerful talent development program at the MDP, LDP and EDP levels to accelerate the ACHIEVEMENT process into winning organizations - https://www.jeffreymagee.com/leadership-academy.cfm).

Suffice it to say, the utilization of performance enhancement resources and tools already available within your organization should be massively deployed universally, consistently and regularly to combat the rogue employee that can implode a team and organization.

1. Performance Review documents should be executed as a starting memorialization point-in-time with significant KPI detail; It is a perfect pre-approved document that your organization has created to show all players where the performance bars are and standards-of-conduct lie, so grab this instrument and have an impromptu performance review and score the problematic behavior accordingly; many times when someone actually sees that their behavior is being documented, scored and memorialized, this can serve as a massive wake-up call.

2. Performance Development Plan (PDP), should be immediately reviewed for multiple KPIs that are being failed at, by this "terrorist" player; Use your annual PDP and refine it so as to be executed for the intermediate and long-term performance adjustments, behavior expectations and attitudinal changes with significant detail.

3. Performance Improvement Plan (PIP) 1:1 Coaching check-ins on progress should be maintained, monitored, documented and addressed with significant detail accordingly on a weekly basis for the first 30, 60, 90 days; This is the most critical documentation and developmental tool at your disposal to be used; Once created, it must be entered into their permanent personnel file, no second chances are to be offered or tolerated, and for management to fail on this activity is paramount to sending a signal that it is open season to be a "Terrorist" and an even louder signal to your "Transformers" and Peak Performer Rock Stars that they are actually not respected, appreciated or valued – you will see a commensurate and proportional reduction in their performance when they see that you have no spine to deal with "Terrorists".

4. The gravity of the toxic behavior and/or passive-aggressive behavior should also be noted by your HR Team and also engaged as a secondary reinforcement for the supervising manager's efforts with significant discussion and detail.

Document to grow and document to terminate …. If someone chooses to be the antithesis of the TALENTification process, free up the future to enjoy opportunities elsewhere!

As suggested earlier in this book, you should also consider the multitude of social medial platforms today that talent organizations can access and provide you critical insight data in evaluating a prospective new addition to your organization, if you did this, review those analytics for insights as to how best to integrate the team to the new player and the new player to the team. Likewise, you should review the social media footprint a person has now for insights of what makes them excited, that you can leverage to better integrate them to individuals on your team. And look back over the past year or so to ensure that critical information was not missed in the interviewing and vetting process, that may be valuable now in the on-boarding and integration steps of the TALENTfication process.

Unless the business of your business is missionary work or charity, a business's job is not to employ those who do not have the organization's best interest and welfare in mind. Everyone will greatly appreciate the absence of what has evolved as non-human capital. A central theme of the ACHIEVEMENT process is the free-will choices, actions, commitments and behaviors that individuals exhibit; the mad, sad, bad, caustic employee has made their choices. As these individuals typically evolve into a very loud minority that is able to derail the ACHIEVEMENT process by wild threats of HR grievances or litigation – document, terminate and call their bluff; you will never lose!

As a leader and manager, it is your role to take solace in this responsibility – defer to ACHIEVEMENT level 7 for resource tools and discussion responsibilities.

The organization always wins!

As you undertake this important Fifth phase to the ACHIEVE-MENT life cycle, always stay focused on on how this applies to the TALENT in a multitude of applications. For an organization, it demands the understanding of each application and how they actually must align as one for ultimate ROI. Identify at each of the following five TALENT considerations, what you expect the new talent to do, TDR. This must be done first because it leads into the next crucial step: what KSAs are required to perform the role (TDR) you plan to put them in:

1. TALENT management of the INDIVIDUAL;

2. TALENT management of career PATHWAYS;

3. TALENT management of critical essential POSITION pathways;

4. TALENT management of secondary support POSITION pathways; and

5. TALENT management of the ORGANIZATION.

Understanding the life cycle of TALENTification is critical and we hope this book helps synthesize what we know about human capital and provides a simplified approach for individuals and organizations to move beyond the carousel of the past.

Chapter Six

Vest All In The DEI(A) Process

Vest all in the Process – Often in the talent arena, Human Resources either assumes total responsibility or managers defer their responsibility to Human Resources. The most effective organizations have a holistic approach to TALENTization, where many people have equal responsibility to identify and clarify needs, find and acquire the right people, assimilate them into the organization quickly and help them succeed while they are there. Having operational managers and the human resources department equal owners of the organization's talent is essential, and having senior executives engaged and involved with all processes ensures that only the essential activities are focused on. If there was a "silver bullet" for TALENTization, it is that the organization's most important and valuable asset is its people, and that the organization's executives, operational managers, and human resources are all focused on maximizing this asset.

Inclusion is the objective here. The more you can provide individuals with meaningful opportunities to share, learn, grow and serve, the organization will always be the beneficiary. Again, here is where you can task, grow and challenge individuals, business groups, the ERG can be a major champion in the DEI Organizational goal attainment, from both a grassroots level and as proactive players in organizational policy implementation. Provide opportunities for feedback of how people feel DEI is being actualized and always create a climate and culture of solutions whenever problems may be identified. Work hard here to ensure levels of bias (Unconscious, Categorization and Affinity) do not create barriers to success, and identify early and fast any barriers that arise, so they can be addressed.

Consider Employee Resource Groups (ERG) aka Employee Engagement Groups or Diversity Network Groups for individual affinity if appropriate, like: Women's Staff, LGBTQ+, Race Equality, Disabled, Veterans, Parents, Alumni, Customer feedback, Governance, Leadership, Cross-team, etc.

Identify ways to include everyone in activities, socialization, work projects and celebrations, to gain a better respect and appreciation for the diversity among us and the rewards for us.

All next steps aligned with previous KPIs: *Gaining Ownership, Buy-In, Empowerment, Free-Will Engagement, Proactive Mindset & Behaviors; Continuous human-capital growth and challenges; Talent life cycle by Position, Tenure, Individual Aspirations, Organizational Needs, Market Needs and Attrition Needs; Mentoring/Champions; Etc.*

All next steps aligned with previous KPIs - Gaining Ownership, Buy-In, Empowerment, Free-Will Engagement, Proactive Mindset & Behaviors; Continuous human-capital growth and challenges; Talent life cycle by Position, Tenure, Individual Aspirations, Organizational Needs, Market Needs and Attrition Needs; Mentoring/Champions; Etc.

This is a game changer between organizations that just plod along every day, just keeping their head above water as the saying goes and the organizations that are truly best in class. When you require a peer group and the immediate two levels above to be vested in the evaluation, performance review, feedback loops, and accountability documents for performance, it brings a heightened level of engagement among all involved.

When it is recognized that the true brand differentiator today lies within the uniqueness of the human capital one possesses, and, that this talent is your organizational multiplier for success, then one can truly attain levels of performance success and accomplishment never before imagined.

This is a simple, yet involved, phase of the ACHIEVEMENT talent model, as it is predicated on people being able to be message focused, job-responsibility centric and purely performance focused and not be so fixated on personalizing every interaction that it becomes a person centric "gotcha" endeavor. This is about the health of the organization, so that everyone can be assured of an opportunity to participate and to be gainfully employed. If any one person fails, it can have far-reaching ramifications to the organization overall and the talent development futures of everyone.

As presented in Chapter One, all organizational effectiveness and sustained success comes down to five critical factors or elements, the first three being (1) Strategy/Systems; (2) Operations/Procedures; and (3) Tactics/Process. Yet, the only way one truly engages talent, develops talent, retains talent and retires talent is when leaders, talent-management stakeholders and organizations ensure that the last two factors are present: (4) Execution/Talent; (5) and Accountability/Human Capital.

So, when we discuss VESTING all involved, we are not just discussing the first three business-building factors or elements; we are strongly focusing on the last two factors or elements being embraced and owned by all parties involved.

If your organization is facing challenges at any individual level of the ACHIEVEMENT model, you'll know if people are vested, as fewer real problems and challenges raise their head because you have the talent to forecast and foresee more effectively and thereby head off problems before they become disruptive. You also have more opportunities for success than you can manage and people are more apt to be involved and volunteer.

Another great way to ensure and invest all in the process, is to look at your talent pipeline through multiple lenses of humanity. For example, to ensure generational connectedness, encourage or even create a cross-functional group made up of individuals from each major generational demographic, as appropriate to your organization, and/or reach out to clients for continuous feedback on ways to better serve, engage, empower, attract and retain great talent throughout the talent ACHIEVEMENT life cycle. Years ago, I observed many in the talent development arm of an organization, Human Resources, all seemed to be of the same age. It takes concentrated effort to recognize that what drives one generational segment may have no meaning or derail another. So, bring together the Centurions, Baby-Boomers, Generation X/Ys, Millennials, and Generation Zs for input on how your talent endeavors are being received, perceived and actualized. Form and facilitate focus-groups, sounding-boards and outreach opportunities that allow for individuals at every level of your organization to share, learn, brainstorm and offer real-time innovations for continued engagement of your human capital. Involve all in this process, so it becomes second nature for people to strive to want to be involved at their respective levels and in concert with their appropriate Player Capability Index levels.

This same approach can be applied to any vocation, industry, position, ethnicity, gender, etc. If you deem it important, then always make sure you have viable and appropriate representative input(s) from all sides.

You can instill reward mechanisms, as well, throughout the organization to derive a vested interest from all parties, at all levels, for achievement in what one does as a team. Consider Southwest Airlines (at the time of this book publication). At 50 years of age, it is an organization that has posted a profit every year, with the industry's lowest human resources talent problems, complaints, grievances and litigation. An organization where, when an employee has to leave its employment for legitimate reasons, the departing employee is sad. During my work with them, I learned that one of their ways to vest everyone involved and engage with others is in how individuals are compensated; *in essence, the everyone has skin in the game philosophy.* Individuals are compensated for the KPIs of the role they serve. They are compensated when the teams that they are on achieve regular KPI goals. And everyone is compensated at the end of the year if the organization achieves its goals and KPIs. With three levels of compensation offered, the culture and organization are more conducive to teamwork and drawing upon one another's unique talent abilities, rather than only looking out for oneself!

Remember, the overall employee experience is shaped and determined by how you (individually and organizationally) manage your side of each of the ACHIEVEMENT life cycle phases and what the individual employee receives, sees, observes, and internalizes as their EXPERIENCE along the way. Every touchpoint from the organization, whether intentional or unintentional, whether overt or not, still shapes the experience an individual has within the work environment.

Vesting everyone into the process of ACHIEVEMENT and success is critical. It's a trajectory game changer; it's what others may call a pivot point of accelerating to greater levels of excellence, as opposed to merely maintaining daily status quo.

1. Create a culture wherein everyone always strives for excellence.
2. Create an environment wherein it is safe to challenge what others do for greater understanding and potential ways for improvement.

3. Expect from others solutions and ideas when raising a concern, rather than leaving them for others to address and resolve

4. Expect and invite individuals with the KSAs to participate and take lead roles in evaluating everything that is done presently or anything being considered in the future, for additional talent oversight and input.

5. Celebrate other's wins as management and leadership. Your organization will quantifiably morph forward by the combined energies of others, as opposed to the singular efforts of one.

In order to vest everyone in the process, it is critical that ownership is on the side of both the employee and the organization to ensure the process of development and engagement is embraced and owned by everyone.

A key aspect of TALENTification is the responsibility of every supervising manager primarily, and hiring manager secondarily, to be cognizant of what each person on their team does, what their growth goals are, what their growth potential is within that business unit or within the organization overall. Talent gaps, lacks and losses should be ata minimum if the ACHIEVEMENT process is at work. Learning of an impending employee departure because of employment growth opportunities with another employer, whether it is because the employee did not see themselves within your organization or because you failed to articulate your strategic plans for them, is a failure of the TALENTification succession process.

Individuals, likewise, should be aware of the TALENTification process, as well, and should feel comfortable communicating with their supervising manager, hiring manager and senior leaders about the goals/aspirations they have and whether they feel those are being met.

Business/C-Suite leaders at their respective levels must architect out their immediate, intermediate and long-term talent needs, growth migration patterns of personnel and the ongoing professional development needs in order for their business enterprise to survive and thrive – from both the technician skills/aptitudes requirements and professional KSAs -- to perform the TDR expected.

The degree of culture disruption, productivity disruption and profitability hits an organization takes annually due to these failures is massive and on a global basis. Architect out individual player aspirations for positional efficiency, productivity, profitability and development as it relates to the individual ... align this with succession needs.

As you undertake this important Sixth phase of the ACHIEVEMENT life cycle, always stay focused on how this applies to the TALENT in a multitude of applications. For an organization, it demands the understanding of each application and how they actually must align as one for ultimate ROI. Identify at each of the following five TALENT considerations, what you expect the new talent to do, TDR. This must be done first because it leads into the next crucial step: what KSAs are required to perform the role (TDR) you plan to put them in:

1. TALENT management of the INDIVIDUAL;

2. TALENT management of career PATHWAYS;

3. TALENT management of critical essential POSITION pathways;

4. TALENT management of secondary support POSITION pathways; and

5. TALENT management of the ORGANIZATION.

Understanding the life cycle of TALENTification is critical and we hope this book helps synthesize what we know about human capital and provides a simplified approach for individuals and organizations to move beyond the carousel of the past.

Chapter Seven

Enhance Through DEI(A)

Development & Management

Enhance Through Development & Management – With great talent acquired, integrated and onboarded, assimilated into their role and team so they are engaged, the next focus area is to manage their performance so they can excel and to develop them throughout their career with the organization. Effective performance management is critical for excellence and for creating a bench of leaders to allow the organization to continue to grow and replace senior leaders over time. Development of talent has a dual purpose: One is to continue to advance skills for a person's current role and the other is to prepare them for future roles, whether lateral or a promotion, or whether in the same region or global.

To grow your DEI talent, consider creating job experiences that have stretch assignment, opportunities to work cross diversity lines and inclusion with talent that some would otherwise never cross paths with. Mento both new talent, peer-to-peer talent and establish reverse Mentor opportunities for younger or diverse talent to engage the established talent within an organization. Consider how often you provide structured formal and informal performance reviews? Within these opportunities consider creating additional assessment questions to gather feedback on individuals perspective on DEI initiatives, processes, programs and opportunities from their user experience.

All next steps aligned with previous KPIs: *Pipeline flow of Human Capital on a daily/weekly/monthly basis; Deployment of six core Managerial, Leadership, Coaching, Motivation Interventions (via the Managerial-Leadership-Coaching L-Grid™); Managing Career Pathing; Effective and timely developmental Performance Assessments or Reviews for growth optics; Facilitation of regular legitimate meaningful Professional Development Plans and, as/when appropriate, Professional Improvement Plans; Discussions tied to Career-Pathing; AI is a player; TALENT Horizon Report - Succession Development Span-of-Influence Chart; Etc.*

The sign of great leadership and organizations is when they can grow great people, afford to lose them into the community as immediate contributors for and to others, and elevate their existing internal talent to keep right on going, not losing one heartbeat in the transition.

Managing the performance of talent can be a daunting endeavor, and yet, it can be managed with clarity of purpose and effective use of talent-development and management tools. One way to ensure the integrity of your talent pipeline is to ensure that your environment and culture is calibrated for sustained success. For example, every organization of any size should consider having a working, robust Organizational/Employee Handbook that derives from the core Values of the organization and details how individuals are to operate, act, conduct themselves and behave. It is more than just the organization's procedures and standard-of-conduct guidelines, this document should lay the groundwork for every Job Description, and both should be aligned with the organization's Performance Assessment/Review documents. These three sets of documents should all be designed, maintained and updated with one another in mind.

Think of it this way in evaluating your talent operations:

1. *Organizational/Employee Handbook:* stipulates this is what we are.

2. The *Job Description* stipulates this is what you are here to own.

3. The *Performance Assessment/Review* stipulates this is how we are measuring performance success expected from you.

Clarity and detail in each document calibrates how human resourcing, talent management and organization leaders execute daily, weekly, monthly, Quarterly and annual work product and talent integration, management, development and success overall.

In developing each individual within your organization, consider having both individuals and their managing supervisor evaluate each variable within the Player Capability Index Model (as presented in Chapter Two) on a regular basis, as it relates to their Job Description and performance growth needs. Detail out annual PDPs against the Player Capability Index Model and consider not just designing that individual's annual PDP for their job, also calibrate against where you and that individual see their role growing within the organization.

Each core responsibility of one's Job Description can serve notice for action items within a PDP, as it relates to what one can do to maintain performance excellence in each area; what one can do to improve upon performance excellence; and, as it relates to areas of growth and improvement needs, to perform at a level of excellence. The more detailed the KPIs are, the more engaged talent can be at every level. Other indicators of PDP criteria also should have data competition points, accountability references, peer or supervisory checkpoints, and pay-offs for talent attainment.

Think of the chain metaphor: a chain is only as strong as its weakest _____? Well, that is conversely accurate in that a chain is only as strong as its *strongest* link. And every link represents individual talent in an organization; talent management is about making every link and, thus, every person as strong as possible.

The management and development of talent within an organization also must be radically disrupted if true peak performance is to be achieved. Imagine a professional athlete having a talent professional track their every move, collect the analytics, tape them during critical practice and game times, and then holding all that data secret until the end of the season? An annual one time a year sit-down for performance discussion – Crazy.

There would be no talent development and there would be no talent management in this situation – it would be complete chaos and pure luck for any wins, and more probable, greater losses.

Your organization should approach talent development and management as high-performing industry athletes and athletic organizations do. Determine optimal performance minimums and potential performance achievements, and build a talent pipeline around greatness. Build your talent leaders around accepting nothing less, and your organization and culture will create the best. The effective use of talent-assessment tools is critical in developing greatness and should be only one in a myriad of tools and measurements used in talent management, talent development, talent promotion, talent compensation and never used as the sole barometer to advancement and pay raises. That is how this aspect of talent management has been bastardized in past years!

Whether this is done as a 30-, 60-, 90-day talent calibration tune-up or check-in as a part of the initial on-boarding of new talent to ensure success, or you do this on what you determine is a regular basis with all talent, providing real-time measurable feedback on performance is critical to talent development.

An effective Performance Review/Assessment instrument should, along with your specific unique needs, also include core sections and KPIs that communicate what you really need. Consider this template:

1. Measure the behaviors and meaningful actions you need/want;
2. Measure every variable appropriate for peak performance and guard against the behaviors and action that you do not want, as well;

3. Benchmark against HR Metrics used to measure ROI;

4. Benchmark off of organizational Values, Vision & Mission Statement KPIs;

5. Measure if the final instrument creates, builds, reinforces or kills your Culture.

Remember, what gets measured sends the message to individuals of what really matters in the eyes of talent leadership. Here is a template of critical talent measurement areas I have gleaned from decades of work with my Fortune 100 Clients, leading industry trade associations and more importantly, the entrepreneurial leaders in the mid-cap size business place. You can add as appropriate and adjust this template accordingly to have the measurements you need for talent overall and in specific Job Description areas, as well.

What you also recognize as unique to this proposed template model from standard assessments, is that there is a mathematical score for each area. That the annotated action notes or PDP notes are logged in individually at each measurement section and not in one global macro-annotated action PDP note at the end of the mathematical measurements – that is too cumbersome to do in one place and tends to be far less informational, instructional and more vague in any attempt to really grow your talent.

Likewise, on my model, there is a large L-Grid on the top right corner of the Performance Review/Assessment instrument; that will be addressed later in this Chapter. The L-Grid has a direct correlation to all of the data that you chronicle in the Performance Review/Assessment instrument and vice versa.

You can always challenge your Performance Review/Assessment instrument against feedback from your existing talent population and their previous employer's tools, and/or against any industry Trade Association or affiliations that you have and tools that they can provide, as well. Get this step in the talent development and management process right and you will build a strong talent pool at every level within your organization right through to your C-Suite bench!

Part I: Goal Setting – *What you need to achieve.*

Part II: Review of Employee Job Description – *What you do*

Part III: Behavioral Traits and Performance Factors – *How you behave.*

Performance Review & Development Assessment

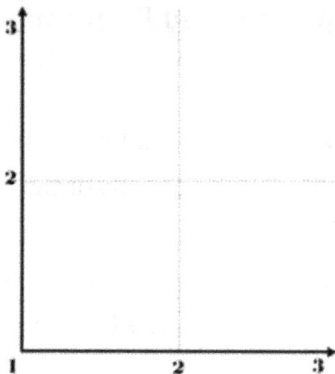

Employee Name: _____

Job Title: _____

Evaluation Period: _____ to _____

Supervisor: _____

Peer Reviewer: _____

Grid for management use

Part I: Goal Setting – What you need to achieve

List the 3-5 target goals, objectives, projects, or special assignments to be achieved or worked on in the next assessment period.

Part II: Review of Employee Job Description – What you do

Review the employee's job description and make comments based on defined areas of responsibility. What does the employee excel at? In what area(s) is more training or better performance needed? Be sure the entire job description has been accounted for.

Part III: Behavioral Traits and Performance Factors- How You Behave

Listed below are behavioral traits and performance factors that are key to the success of the employee in his or her position. The following rating system will be used. **Any line item marked "Needs Improvement" must have a plan of action toward improving the skill attached to this assessment. Line items marked "Exceeds**

Expectations" must include some examples of how expectations were exceeded. Please type "Plans of Action" and "Exceeding Expectation" examples in a different colored font immediately following the specific trait or performance factor.

1. **Needs Improvement** – Consistently or occasionally fails to meet job-description requirements due to performance, behavior, or lack of knowledge. Immediate improvement required to maintain employment.

2. **Meets Expectations** – Able to perform 100% of job-description requirements and duties satisfactorily. Normal guidance and supervision are required.

3. **Exceeds Expectations** – Frequently exceeds job description requirements; all planned objectives were achieved above the established standards and accomplishments were made in unexpected areas.

General Performance
Rating

- **PUNCTUALITY** – Employee observes assigned work hours and adheres to them.

- **ATTENDANCE** – Employee can be depended on to report to work regularly with few unplanned absences. Provides proper notification when absent.

- **POLICIES & PROCEDURES** – Employee understands and complies with company policies and procedures.

- **JUDGMENT & DECISION-MAKING** – Employee effectively analyzes problems, determines appropriate action for solutions, and exhibits timely and decisive action; thinks logically.

- **DEPENDABILITY** – Employee can be depended upon to apply him/herself to tasks, use time efficiently, follow instructions and carry out assignments to completion.

- **PROFESSIONALISM & WORK HABITS** – Employee demonstrates pride in the job and conducts self in a professional manner; identifies with the mission of the company.

- **INITIATIVE** – Employee accepts and/or volunteers for extra responsibilities beyond normal job duties in order to improve self. Employee monitors projects independently and follows through appropriately.

- **DRESS** – Employee's workplace attire is professional (business casual, at a minimum). When onsite at a company event or at a client company, employee's dress is professional and matches the expectations of the client.

  WORK SPACE – Employee maintains a professional, neat, and operational work space.

Job Performance & Knowledge

Rating

- **QUALITY OF WORK** – Employee demonstrates accuracy, neatness, and thoroughness in performing job duties.

- **QUANTITY OF WORK** – Employee demonstrates ability to meet required work output without sacrificing quality; ability to manage several responsibilities simultaneously.

- **SENSE OF URGENCY** – Employee demonstrates a sense of professional urgency in meeting their job responsibilities and interacting with others.

- **JOB KNOWLEDGE** – Employee possesses and demonstrates necessary knowledge and skills to accomplish job duties. Uses experience effectively to enhance work performance.

- **TIME MANAGEMENT & ORGANIZATIONAL SKILLS** – Employee demonstrates ability to effectively plan, organize, and prioritize work; demonstrates effective use of time-management practices; completes tasks in a timely manner and meets deadlines without sacrificing quality.

- **TRAINING & SELF IMPROVEMENT** – Employee utilizes what is learned in training; makes an effort to obtain on-the-job training and to improve skills and knowledge for advancement and improved performance.

- **ONGOING TRAINING & SELF IMPROVEMENT** – Employee seeks continued opportunities for additional learning and training; makes an effort to obtain on-the-job training and to improve skills and knowledge for advancement and improved performance.

- **ADAPTABILITY** – Employee adjusts with ease to changes in duties, procedures, supervisors, or work environment. Employee accepts new ideas and approaches to work; responds appropriately to constructive criticism and suggestion for work improvement.

- **CREATIVITY/INNOVATION** – Employee demonstrates new and creative ideas in carrying out job duties and makes constructive suggestions for seeking new and improved procedures.

- **SELF MANAGEMENT** – Demonstrates good self discipline. Has the ability to forecast needs and opportunities and proactively exercises abilities to capitalize on those opportunities. Has the ability to be productive (not just busy) to attain continued profitability and productivity.

Interpersonal Relationships & Communication

Rating

- **ATTITUDE**– Employee demonstrates cooperative attitude with fellow employees and a willingness to share responsibilities as part of the team; displays a positive attitude toward work and fellow employees.

- **RELATIONSHIP W/ SUPERVISOR** – Employee responds positively to supervision, direction, and constructive criticism.

- **DEALING W/ THE PUBLIC** – Employee demonstrates tact and patience in dealing with others. Relationship with clients is firm but fair, positive, decent, and respectful. Promotes good public relations and works effectively with teammates, clients and vendors alike.

- **WRITTEN COMMUNICATION** – Employee demonstrates a high level of competency in written expression, including reports and correspondence; uses grammar and syntax correctly and expresses ideas clearly and succinctly.

- **VERBAL COMMUNICATION** – Employee demonstrates competency in oral expression and listening; expresses thoughts clearly; listens and understands oral instructions and information and actions reflect that understanding.

- **OPEN COMMUNICATION** – Employee interacts with peers and supervisors in such a manner that good rapport is maintained with the company; follows established chain-of-command.

The following section is for employees in a Customer Service & Sales role.

Rating

- **RELATIONSHIP BUILDING** – Employee has made routine contact with Centers of Influence (also known as advocates, allies, and champions) to make sure the company's name is top of their mind and to ensure the Manager has a pulse on market trends and issues that sales reps are facing.

- **LEAD GENERATION** – Employee has worked to grow his/her market share through additional market contacts since last assessment period.

- **SELLING PROCESS** – Employee understands the selling process and has worked to ensure effective selling is taking place and that their skills of and the skills of others have been elevated since the last assessment period.

- **MAINTAINS A CHAMPION SELLING ATTITUDE** – Employee demonstrates, promotes and exudes a positive selling attitude and motivational beliefs.

- **PHONE MANAGEMENT** – Employee manages calls efficiently and meets expected inbound and outbound call volumes.

- **DATABASE MANAGEMENT** – Employee keeps their contact files updated and current and documents thoroughly what they have done for each contact. Call back dates are maintained and current.

Supervisory Skills

This section to be completed only for those who perform supervisory functions within the company (in addition to the previous sections).

Rating

- **UNDERSTANDING OF DUTIES** – Supervisor understands the duties, functions, and responsibilities of their management position and the role they play on the team; understands the mission of the company and adequately represents position of management.

- **LEADERSHIP SKILLS** – Supervisor demonstrates leadership qualities by setting an example of excellence and dedication for subordinates to follow; motivates subordinates to perform duties to optimum level of abilities.

- **EFFECTIVE SUPERVISION** – Supervisor manages subordinates effectively in order to maximize their performance and produce the desired quantity and quality of work; exerts authority when necessary.

- **ORGANIZATIONAL SKILLS** – Supervisor demonstrates effective use of organizational skills in order to keep department and subordinates working in a cohesive and organized manner; good knowledge of all aspects of work of department.

- **RELATIONSHIP W/ SUBORDINATES** – Supervisor has an open-door policy with subordinates; deals with all in a fair and impartial manner.

- **INTERPERSONAL SUPERVISORY SKILLS** – Supervisor demonstrates effective interpersonal relationship practices with peers, subordinates, and management, so as to foster good communication within the department and company; effectively and properly uses the chain of command.

- **STAFF** – Supervisor is accessible to his/her staff and others during work hours and beyond (when emergencies arise). He/she has regular team briefings, meetings, and communication as appropriate. Supervisor effectively promotes the improvement and development of staff and subordinates through formal training sessions, coaching, and other activities.

- **SELF DEVELOPMENT** – Employee demonstrates a proactive behavior in searching out job-appropriate skills training (books, articles, audio, video, live classes, etc.) during the assessment period to elevate his/her competency level to share and guide the team to greater successes.

- **BUDGET RESPONSIBILITIES** – Supervisor has a firm grasp of the budgeting process and how to analyze and use the data to impact the profitability of his/her division.

Personal/Professional Development

This section addresses specific personal/professional developmental commitments for the next measurement-assessment period.

- **PROFESSIONAL DEVELOPMENT** – To better develop and grow professionally overall within your organization, I plan to…

- **POSITIONAL DEVELOPMENT** – To better develop and grow my Positional/Job/Rank effectiveness, in the areas of Technical and Professional capabilities/proficiency, I plan to enroll in the following programs, classes, webcasts/seminars, distance learning, certifications, programs, or books to be read, or journals to subscribe to, etc.

- **PERSONAL DEVELOPMENT** – To better develop and grow I plan to…

Signatures

Supervisor: _____

Date: _____

I have been advised of my performance ratings. I have discussed the contents of this review with my supervisor. My signature does not necessarily imply agreement. My comments are as follows (optional).

Employee Signature: _____

Date: _____

The implementation of such talent measurement and talent-development tools, such as this Performance Review/Assessment instrument or any other such tool, can be executed as a Peer Review, Self-Review or Rater/Supervisor Review. It can be completed and reviewed by the rating supervisor and their supervisor before being administered to the receiving talent in question. This makes for a learning and developmental opportunity for the two levels of leadership before it is presented to the assessed individual. It also allows the senior leader to engage and hold the rating supervisor accountable for the documentation and scores. This allows the two levels of leaders to grow and develop themselves at a new talent level, if in fact, the ultimate aim of Performance Review/Assessment instruments is to ensure talent measurement and development is fair, objective and accurate at every level – good or bad.

In driving home your organization's intent and commitment to TALENTification as an essential thread throughout your organization, you might want to consider incorporating your organization's VALUES into your personal performance assessment instruments. This could raise a new level of emphasis, concentration and focus by every individual within a work group area or across the organization in entirety. By assessing and measuring how individuals live the organization's VALUES, this allows you to address behaviors and actions that lead to TALENTification successes and creates an atmosphere of internal self-reflection as to whether individuals are showcasing 24/7 their best talent or worst example of themselves.

In many situations, talent assessment, and thus, talent development is not a serious endeavor. What tends to happen is people are afraid to have honest or tough talks with colleagues and staff within an organization. Everyone knows when subpar talent is being allowed to survive and everyone knows when great talent is being abused, taken advantage of and outright screwed. In such a system, the buddy system, nepotism and covering up for subpar players is how you build winning teams. And in fact, such practices become the cancer to every once great organization.

I had one nationally branded client that illuminated this to such a level it was shocking. Instead of holding individuals accountable to their failed performance, documenting it, and engaging them with a developmental trajectory, they instead chose to allow them to transfer out of that specific branch of the organization to another state. Then, once in place in a senior leader role, they imploded that position to such levels of ineptness, one had to go back nearly 50 years to find such levels of failure. But again, because rating supervisors and leaders failed to do their job, talent that was proficient left the organization, mediocre non-talent stayed, and the leader in question was promoted once again.

Back in home-state operations, he was installed into a role in which the immediate predecessor had improved the company's standing from last place in the nation to number two in 18 months. This new underwhelming leader was able to take this number-two-rated business unit and run it off the cliff and back to #50 during his two-year reign. Due to a complete failure at every level of the ACHIEVE-MENT model up to this Chapter, you guessed it, this individual now having two massively quantifiable failures was not retired or fired (which his performance had well-earned), he was once again promoted. Promoted out of his state operations to the national head-quarters level, he could now share his massively failed, flawed, and inept opinions. He influenced how the entire organization nation-ally operated, and you guessed it, more chaos and failure ensued. Due to a complete breakdown in the talent-management process, talent-management personnel, and lack of any rearview mirror an-alytics, failure became a perpetual reality. And because of inade-quate talent development, talent management, talent documenta-tion, talent accountability, this individual was promoted and trans-ferred to join a national headquarters team with two other individ-uals who were even more massively failed than he. Within twelve short months they were able to implode the entire organization, na-tionally, to fail its mission.

All of this was compounded by the actual assessment instruments that rating supervisors used. In the lower-level roles, the assessment instruments were very detailed and allowed for quantitative data be traced and documented objectively (constructively and critically) on individuals. Yet as positions ascended upwards, assessment instruments became far more macro in nature, allowing for subjectivity to creep in, and most alarming, all of the core organizational values and performance expectations disappeared. This lead to massive ineptness taking over. In one anecdotal situation, a mid-level manager was submitting an evaluation on one of their direct reports, scoring them universally at average and acceptable, etc. The senior rater, needing to sign off on this assessment engaged in a discussion about all of said employee's shortcomings in the past year and the problems he created. The senior-level manager told the mid-level manager that if he was to sign off on this inaccurate assessment, then he, the senior rater, would ensure that the mid-level manager's annual assessment reflected his inability to do his job ... What would the mid-level rater/manager like the senior-level rater/leaders to do?

The mid-level manager got the powerful message; not engaging your team individually to grow them, develop them, and counsel them does your team an injustice and the organization a disservice, both now and in the future.

So, the lack of talent trajectory touchpoints to grow and hold individuals accountable at the front line and executive line, can create massive talent issues throughout an organization.

With a newly gained healthy attitude geared for peak performance, talent interaction with others can be elevated to a new level of effectiveness. For many managers, management deals with knowing what results need to be attained, and then focusing energies on available resources to make this magic act happen. In the course of working toward immediate, intermediate, and long-term results, traditional (old-school) management focuses upon who is most effective at barking out directions, giving orders, and maintaining significant degrees of power by controlling resources.

To truly attain peak performance personally and professionally, management in the future needs to recognize that there are six completely different ways to interact with others daily to facilitate (lead) the directional growth of and production needed from their personnel assets. A better understanding of the six core styles of managerial leadership (or coaching approaches) will show a management member how to alternate these styles to obtain optimum results (from a team, individual player, and oneself), thereby becoming an effective leader and avoiding micromanagement.

The six alternative management styles are profiled on the following pages. A successful management player in a winning organization must recognize that only one style of managerial leadership intervention can be efficiently utilized at any one time.

Think of these talent management styles as hats on a hat rack inside your organizational walls. You must first take off your personal hat when you come in the door each morning, thereby becoming more objective and less subjective. Then assess the environment to determine which management hat to take from the hat rack and place on your head. Remember, only one hat can be on your head at a time. To maximize your management capabilities, you will continually be taking hats off and putting them on. You must become fluid in these actions. In doing so, you reduce interaction time with players, stimulate greater interactions, and ultimately, see a significant increase in team productivity and positive attitude. This means less management stress and increased management productivity during the traditional daily working hours, less early-morning and late-night work to maintain the status quo.

Breaking down management into six subcategories is easy when you recognize that each day management personnel participates in (or should participate in) only six activities. If management doesn't recognize its six basic alternative styles of intervention, then no matter how hard it works, management will feel as if they are holding on for a fall (and frustration) every day.

Effective managerial leadership is knowing when to put on the correct management hat; by doing so, the leader within you will shine. The six alternate management styles (or hats) are:

1. Manager

2. Teacher

3. Coach

4. Counselor

5. Disciplinarian

6. Mentor

Prior to analyzing the six managerial leadership styles, consider the traditional dictionary definition of management. Traditional and old-style management closely resembles the following definition:

Man-age, v. i. To direct or carry on business affairs; to achieve one's purpose; to exercise executive, administrative, and supervisory direction of a business.

To better understand the roles and responsibilities of each management style, see Table 4.1. Notice the traits common to some of the styles, and the differing traits as well. Based on leadership alternatives, you can assess the whys of some recent interactions and why those management interactions were less productive than desired.

From a talent-development and talent-management perspective, proper engagement can lead to faster wins. Reduce your work and increase results by using less autocratic methods of management. Consider the following six alternative styles of interaction as your initial Six-Block management options:

Table 7.1 Six Alternative Management Styles/6-Block Model

Management Style (Hat)	Responsibilities/Traits
Manager	Hands-on Training (OTJ) Education Rule(s) regulation Knowledge transfer Appraisal evaluator
Teacher	Hands-on Educator as SME Patient to engage
Mentor	Hands-on (5-levels of engagement) Elementary: Educator of basics Secondary: Application

	Post-Secondary: Opportunities Master: PR Agent/Advocate Reverse: Now the Mentee can Mentor
Counselor	Hands-on Serious Problem One-on-one in private Advisor of unacceptable behaviors Pain Factor Motivator Major leverage Solution oriented May or may not document
Disciplinarian	Hands-on Ditto "Counselor" intervention Last Chance/No more discussions Massive documentation time
Coach	Hands-off Attitude adjuster Encourager/focuser Calming factor Personal Cheerleader Education reminder Guider & navigator

The power of management's effectiveness rests in your ability to determine precisely what role needs to be assumed at any given time to obtain organizational results and success from each person you engage on an individual basis. It is critical to the success, productivity, and development of the players that someone at the management level understands that the six core styles are defined and distinguishably different from one another.

For an organization to attain peak performance, management needs to assess daily environments and the players within those environments to determine how much time needs to be invested in any one specific management style.

For management to be truly effective, it needs to assume all six core management styles and alternate them routinely to obtain results. Those players vested with the six responsibilities must understand the essence of each. Explore in greater detail the thrust of each management style within your environment and let the following six management subsections serve as a guide to effective leadership alternatives.

Manager

The *manager* is the person who watches out to ensure that organizational rules, policies, procedures, best practices, and guidelines are being followed and addressed. Within this management style, structured training and education of the players is established and executed.

The enforcement of these standards is the primary responsibility of the manager. This position is the most time-consuming. When the manager hat is being worn, the manager must avail herself of the employee, player, or other person, often becoming tied down with interaction(s) with specific players. Therefore, she has limited time available for interfacing with other players on the team, or for focusing energies on other tasks charged specifically to the manager. Traditional management focuses (and is followed up by academic disciplines that focus) efforts on a manager being merely a manager. Organizations that desire to grow and survive in the future need more than managers. Other styles of management are required.

As long as a member of the management team focuses her energies solely on being a manager, the ultimate result is a team being held back from attaining peak performance, increased player tension, organizational frustration, and higher levels of employee turnover than necessary.

In management, the role of manager is the most labor intensive one a player can assume. As long as management focuses on being managers, there will be players on the team (transformers and even more positive transmitters/followers; Gallup Organization's 56 percent) who are ignored, while management is tied down with problem players (terrorists; Gallup Organization's 15 percent) or engaged in the micromanagement of everyone's activities.

Another major drawback to the traditional manager style is that managers are charged by the organization with ensuring that things get done. This philosophy inherently holds back both organizations and players. Most managers focus their efforts on *how* things are being worked on, addressed, completed, and done. This is a dangerous word (and a management concern) for the future. Focusing on the word *how* in today's business world is a self-destructive route. Each time a manager uses the word *how* with another player, she may create an opportunity of automatically provoking a mental fight with that player. With some players this mental challenge is seen in an external outburst, tension, conflict, anger, or hostility in the work-place.

The reason for this is simple. Society has been conditioned (especially via the media for 50 years!) that it is acceptable to challenge another's intellectual position and opinion on issues and things in general. When you use the word *how*, you are challenging another person's position and asserting that yours is better and more sound than theirs -- instant mental challenge and conflict!

There are certainly times when something needs to be done a certain way (how). Successful management realizes that the best (and least threatening) way to communicate this message is to replace *how* with words such as *what* and *why*. The word *how* sounds threatening to another person's ear. Even if management doesn't intend it to be a threat, it still is! Consider the following:

- "That is not how I asked you to…"
- "We don't do it that way. Here is how I…."
- "Let me show you how."

All these statements are offered hundreds of times daily, and more than likely, are not intended to be negative or confrontational. Yet, to the listener they are threatening.

To communicate the what and why requires that management flex its style, and alternate styles as necessary. to accomplish objectives.

Whether you are practicing the alternative styles outlined in order to be a manager, teacher, mentor, counselor, disciplinarian, or coach, you can make the statements above without the "how." This will change the potentially negative interaction into educational player interaction. Consider these statements:

- "I can appreciate what you have done here. What we need to focus on is..."
- "Here is why we need to complete the project according to these specifications..."
- "To save you time, let me show you what I need..."

Other alternative management styles to adapt and adopt are teacher, mentor, counselor, disciplinarian, and coach.

Teacher

As a *teacher* your management style is similar in many respects to the manager's but goes deeper. The critical difference is that when one deploys the teacher style, there is a greater need for deeper education and training to take place due to an individual's lack of functional knowledge to do the tasks required for his position. So along with the teacher needing to have a command of the "elementary knowledge" in which he will be teaching, training, and educating another, he must also be very patient in interactions with the other person. The patience is necessary. When teaching elementary knowledge, an individual can implode the interaction if he is not willing to take a calmer, more easygoing, and more patient approach to the intervention. For the Type A driver personalities, this would imply the need to take some mental Valium before engaging the other person!

Mentor

Another management style is that of *mentor*. While this is also a hands-on, labor-intensive style, it does not mean management actually serves as the mentor, although it can. Key players on the team at any level can augment the manager's efforts by serving in this valuable position. There are some basic requirements for a mentor to have successful interactions and a professional relationship with another colleague or team player.

The key here is to be accessible for the mentee, yet not micromanage the relationship. Here is where you default to instruments like a PDP to engage the mentee where he is and chart a developmental and sequential path to achieving his aspirations or helping him to grow and become a viable candidate for consideration and selection for higher-level roles in the organization.

Management needs to assess the ability of each player individually (via the Managerial Coaching Engagement L-Grid Model (aka SA for skill/attitude) presented later in this chapter, along with techniques presented in subsequent chapters). A primary function of individuals in managerial leadership positions is to determine which players can be assisted to greater levels of productivity by assigning mentors. When an individual or a team possesses good functional knowledge of the job and maintains a healthy attitude/perspective toward it, a mentor would be the go-to person to make performances excel.

Players on a team who could be tapped to serve as mentors could be transformers of any age and capacity within the organization.

Mentors need to be patient, sage people who are willing to share their learned experiences and knowledge freely with wanting individuals. An effective mentor divorces emotions from the situation and serves to educate and expand a player's ability and knowledge base, through hands-on interaction (based upon the mentor's own experiences of success and failure), simple compatibility, and show-and-tell with the person being mentored. The players on the team need to know there is someone they can turn to, confide in, and gain direction and support from in the absence of their managers and coaches.

Developing players into mentors is also a powerful way to stimulate valuable interaction from senior-level players on a team that may be burning out and slowing down. Older players can serve as great organizational champions if used genuinely and strategically within the overall management structure.

The role of mentor is a powerful one, as outlined in Table 7.2. The mentor is, in essence, shaping the life of, and building security for the future of, an organization. Choose your mentors wisely and empower them with the resources and support to accomplish your objectives.

Table 7.2 Five Different Mentor Styles/Types: The Mentor Life Cycle

Elementary mentor	A mentor who serves as an educator and teacher to the person being mentored. This style of mentoring provides the person being mentored with the basics and "how-tos."
Secondary mentor	The person being mentored has graduated and knows the "how-tos" and now needs a motivator, encourager, or coach to show him greater functional applications of knowledge in the environment he works within.
Post-secondary mentor	The person being mentored now knows and is performing. Now, he needs someone to bring him along and serve as his champion and keep building and reinforcing his confidence level(s). This level of mentoring serves to direct the efforts in a specialized way for peak performance and maximum contribution to an organization.
Master mentor	This mentor serves as the sponsor for the person being mentored and promotes his/her abilities to others. The mentor serves as the PR

	representative. The mentor finishes polishing the person being mentored here and prepares her for the next level or mentor life cycle.
Reverse mentoring	Now the person who was mentored repays the organization by sharing the knowledge and experience gained with someone else. The person being mentored now becomes the mentor and starts the cycle/process all over.

<u>Counselor</u>

Not as glamorous as a management position, yet critical to an organization's ultimate success and team attitude, is the style known as the *counselor*. When considering the deployment of this interaction or intervention style, consult with your human resource professional or legal counsel as appropriate, as there is a heightened likelihood that people that you assess in this need state (and the disciplinarian need state) have the capacity to play victim and may find a sympathetic ear with fellow ignorant individuals. But do not abdicate; forward focus is necessary.

The management cliché "out of sight, out of mind," unfortunately, does not apply here. While management tries to ignore a difficult and unpleasant situation or player, everyone else on that team will know exactly what is going on, and more importantly, who is getting away with what. Consequently, when management does decide it is time to deal with the negativity, there will be more than just the initial problem at hand. Additional challenges always develop as a result of management inaction.

When a problem surfaces or a difficult player is on a team (as the SA Model illustrates later in this chapter) and management has exhausted all pleasantries and niceties, only one management option is left. That is to assume the role of counselor.

The counselor role can be unpleasant, as this is where management must stand and hold its ground. While limited give-and-take negotiation may be allowed, when a relationship has advanced this far and management has assumed the style of counselor, the worst-case scenario has already been prepared for (living beyond this person's presence on the team). Management must go one-on-one with the problem player (and/or her representative, if your environment is conditioned for such instances).

Things are serious at this point. The player with the challenging or negative behavior or attitude becomes counterproductive to the team and organization and must be dealt with.

It is in engaging an individual in this area that a detailed, behavior-focused PIP should be administered with detailed KPIs for action, detailed next steps for improvement, next-step ramifications for continued unimproved performance, and time dated for execution. As and when appropriate, obviously consult with your organization's HR leadership team for any specific guidance on how to proceed and how to administrate a PIP. If you do not have a staffed HR team, check with your outside HR benefits firm or legal counsel. Alternately, any human resource trade association can provide you with template PIP forms.

If there is any concern with an individual that you are needing intense behavior corrective actions from and DEI, enlist feedback from multiple confidents to ensure that you are being objective, fair and inclusive in what you have done and are about to do.

Here is a template PIP document we use with our clients. This document allows the leader to immediately isolate the unacceptable behavior, actions and attitudes of an employee, and then create an immediate strategy and action plan of KPIs to alter trajectory and get a player on the track towards success once again.

Personal Improvement Plan (PIP)

JeffreyMagee

Employee/Associate
Name _____

Supervisor _____   Date _____

Observer _____

Reason for Counseling	Actions/Experiences	Resources	Target Dates	Ramifications/Penalties
□ Insubordination □ Unsatisfactory Work Performance □ Substance Abuse □ Failure to Follow Instructions □ Unapproved Absence □ Employee Handbook Violation □ Violation of Company Policy □ Violation of Safety Policy □ Destruction of Company Property □ Other:	Disciplinary action taken: □ Verbal Warning □ Written Warning □ Suspension Describe below the situation/incident [date(s), time(s), witnesses]. Attach additional documentation if necessary. Identify the methods of specific action that must be taken.	Resources or people that will support your actions.	Dates and timelines for implementing the plan and follow-up actions.	What will be the next course of action? If failure to take make substantial improvement on employee's behalf does not take place.

This completed document serves multiple organizational dynamics:

1. As a PIP for the player in question with KPIs.
2. It can be used constructively by both labor and management, and serve as an objective document for reference in subsequent Performance Reviews and those associated documents.

Disciplinarian

Everything detailed for consideration and delivery as the counselor would apply in this role as well.

This is the most uncomfortable of all positions. At this juncture, you have no alternatives left for engaging a person. While there has been a substantial investment in time and training, and institutional and industry acclimation with this individual, his/her behaviors have become so cancerous that they must be eliminated.

Meeting with this individual is now a situation of last resort, and the other person must understand the gravity of his/her actions. Significant documentation is provided and created here, with a clear understanding that this will be the last time it will ever be addressed by you and the organization. Having this meeting is held entirely for your benefit and that of the organization. Such encounters are damaging and not held out of any mindset that you care for the employee. Rally your disgust for this session, so the other person and his representation (should you be working in an arcane, union-based organization that protects pathetic, worthless individuals, as opposed to some forward-thinking unions that do hold employees accountable for their actions) will know there is no negotiation room here on your part and no further discussion will be held. You are merely meeting with this person after having worn the counselor hat with no success. If he/she wants to remain on the team, there will be significant behavior change instantly, or he/she will be creating his/her own exit.

A great opening line in this managerial leadership intervention could be, "We are here because of decisions you have made and plans you have refused to adhere to that are not acceptable to this organization…."

Coach

The ultimate goal of management is to assist players in reaching peak performance and to position themselves in the management style of *coach*: there when players need him, off to the side, otherwise, navigating the team.

When management coaches, it can focus its energies on developing the team, meeting needs, and budgeting energies for future successes. Further, when management coaches, it can also concentrate on the responsibilities of management and not worry about what the players are doing or "how" they are doing it. Management at this level realizes that players assume accountability for their own actions. They act as if the organization is their organization, not as if they are merely a part of some sort of large machinery.

When management takes part in coaching, it is actually practicing a hands-off approach to leadership. The players, here, realize that management has its own unique responsibilities; doing a player's job is not one of them.

The primary focus of the coach is to help players maintain mental and physical perspective and focus on goals. The coach is charged with maintaining the proper attitude for a healthy, happy, and productive environment to develop and sustain productivity. The coach is the constant attitude adjuster, motivator, and encourager of peak performance for each individual he comes into contact with.

As management learns from the Managerial/Leadership/Coaching Engagement Model, the ultimate objective is to advance each player in his own way to the quadrant which puts each in a mentor position for future growth and daily effectiveness. In this way, the manager can build his bench for the position of coach. He can strategically interact, as needed, and assist each player individually for ultimate growth and success.

Reduce your management workload by coaching the team to success and not worrying about being a hands-on manager. By being able to determine what management style (or hat) is required at any given time, you can substantially reduce your interaction time and workload.

Recognizing what position a player, colleague, or customer is in at any given time determines which management style is required and lets you know when and how to increase your level of interaction effectiveness. One technique or model you can utilize to determine where a player is, and therefore, which management hat you need to put on, is the SA Model.

Every player is operating professionally within a need level; they are always in need of something to maximize their potential. As you review the six alternative management styles from Table 7.1 (mentally or physically), recognize that only one style should be used at a time.

By identifying what need level a person has, you can more quickly identify which style to use, reducing your interaction time while increasing your interaction effectiveness and talent engagement.

To determine the managerial/leadership need level of another person and how best to engage them to avoid micromanagement and miscommunication, consider two simple variables. First, assess the skill level (knowledge, education, training, skill set) on the vertical axis from low (score as a zero) to high (score as a ten), with the middle area (score as a five) representing the difference between acceptable and unacceptable skill or aptitude levels. Second, assess the attitude level (desire, motivation, willingness, ownership, acceptance, demeanor, emotions, attitude) on the horizontal axis from low (zero) to high (ten), with the middle area (five) representing the difference between acceptable and unacceptable attitude levels.

For clarity in talent interactions, review the Managerial/Leadership/Coaching Engagement Model illustrated in Figure 7.3 and plot a few of your present players mentally on it as to their overall skill and attitude on your team. Once you have plotted a few players (transmitters, transformers, terrorists), you will recognize the need level or managerial-leadership style for them.

1. Plot high to low on the vertical axis line the skill/aptitude level of the player, as

2. associated with an issue in your mind.

3. Plot left to right on the horizontal axis line the attitude level of the player, as associated with that issue and in your relationship on this specific issue.

4. Now put initials in the appropriate quadrant (box) where these marks intersect.

With a more detailed *Managerial/Leadership/Coaching Engagement Model,* you can determine with greater mathematics where someone may land on the vertical axis or horizontal axis at any situational micro-moment in time, as well as where someone may land from a more macro, overall perspective. You could also explain this to employees, or members of your team, and have them self-assess from their self-awareness perspective. And then benchmark your score with theirs for managerial leadership interventions.

Figure 7.3 Managerial-Leadership-Coaching Engagement Model L-Grid (aka SA Model) Provides a 6-Block of Leadership Intervention Options

Managerial-Leadership-Coaching Engagement Model

This model looks at your ability and attitude, and from that it determines whether you're in need of a coach, mentor, counselor, manager, disciplinarian, or teacher. Please rank yourself using values of 1-10 on both your ability and your attitude. The graph will automatically plot the points. The person who is currently your manager you will rank you as well.

	Attitude	Ability
My Perspective	9	8
Manager's Perspective	6	5

Engagement Model

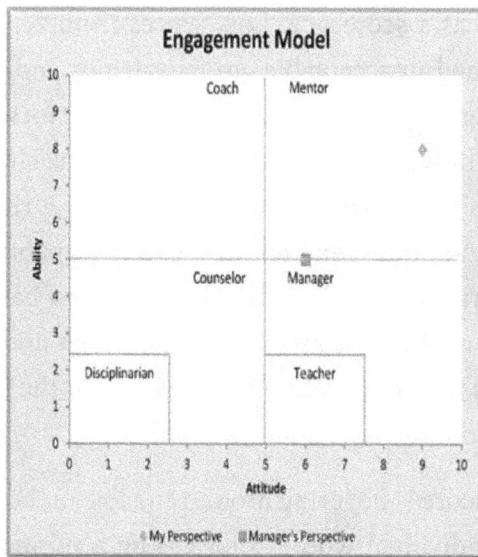

To hold yourself or others on your management-leadership team accountable, use Figure 7.3 (request an excel spreadsheet version through Jeffrey Magee at DrJeffSpeaks@aol.com) and date stamp it once a week or once a month. Assess all your direct reports, employees, team members, and peers on the chart from a macro perspective.

Then, based upon which of the 6-Blocks to leadership assessment and engagement an individual is plotted into, you can track your commitment to engaging them and see how they progress throughout the Managerial/Leadership/Coaching Engagement Model from one assessment period to the next. This also holds both you and them accountable to actionable behaviors to ensure everyone is always growing, thriving, and contributing.

View the diagnostics of both the vertical (Skill, Aptitude, Ability) and horizontal (Attitude, Work Ethic, Passion, Engagement) axis lines as a scorecard. Low scores from zero through 4.9 should be deemed unacceptable, and strategies and actions are necessary to engage the other person to grow them forward on both axis lines. If that movement is not possible, actions should be taken to remove them from that team to another appropriate place within your organization, as long as their Player Capability Index measurements determine that there is real value from having them in the organization. If this is also low and/or a no answer, immediate removal from the organization is necessary for the health and wealth of others and the organization!

If a score is hovering around the five on both axis lines, that reflects an individual who is showcasing a minimum level of acceptance.

Engagement must take place to develop appropriate positional pathway or career pathway improvements with specific KPIs.

The real-time power of this Managerial/Leadership/Coaching Engagement Model is that it can aid you in managing a positive or critical bias of another person, and objectively and diagnostically measure a person's performance against this instrument to determine which engagement style and documentation approach to use. Remember, a superstar may be a tenured member of the team, or it may be the newest or youngest member of the team. True performance effectiveness is not about tenure; it is solely about the value one brings to the team and himself, based upon his ability to deliver. I have met individuals over fifty years of age who came off professional and polished until I applied these analytics and recognized the charlatan in my presence. Likewise, I have had the opportunity to work with twenty somethings who, while they may lack some of the polish that comes with age, are exceedingly proficient and creative members of an organization!

With a firm understanding of how to engage others and attain peak performance, now is the time to proceed forward with an understanding of how these individual interactions play a role in the overall group/team interactions you have.

Diagnostically, there are two powerful ways you can utilize this instrument to assist your managerial leadership engagement style for accelerated talent development and talent management. You can assess individuals for:

1. Immediate intervention needs based upon the situation you face; or

2. Succession planning and succession management purposes for intermediate and long-term success.

The ultimate objective of the Managerial/Leadership/Coaching Engagement Model is to recognize which players are operating in the mentor quadrant. Those players are your high, peak performers and may be viewed as your transformers. The model is also designed to assist you in determining your best course of action (**BCOA**) to motivate and manage every player to eventually rise to the mentor quadrant. And, remember, you don't have to serve as the mentor. It would probably be best left to another to serve in this valuable role. Many studies indicate that you attain maximum mentor/mentored interactions when the mentor is at least two positions removed from the mentored, thus freeing up one of your hands for something else.

Based on the quadrant in which you mentally or physically plot players, colleagues, and superiors, you will gain the needed insight for successful interaction and increased persuasive ability.

For example, imagine you have two alternatives for moving a player in the counselor quadrant toward mentor. One option is for you to move her from counselor to manager/teacher and then, ultimately, to mentor. The problem with this pathway is that it becomes labor-intensive for you as a management option, as manager/teacher means hands-on. A second alternative would be to move the player from counselor to mentor through the coach quadrant, as coach means hands-off. Remember, every decision brings with it another set of decisions and questions, each unique and impacting the ultimate productivity, attitude, and performance levels of you and your organization's team.

In using this 6-Block model, consider the reasons a player may appear in one quadrant one day and in a different quadrant on the next. There are a multitude of management explanations for why players appear in the various SA Model quadrants.

1. A player who lacks proper knowledge or education on an issue, task, project, or subject may procrastinate. Fear factors set in and cause delays in productivity. The player becomes a transmitter, waiting for influence and direction. Your role then becomes that of manager.

2. A player who has a lot of enthusiasm for issues, tasks, and projects may need the subtle push of encouragement. Your role becomes that of a coach.

3. A player who appears on-site as an overeager and power-charged individual can become a loose cannon on the team. While you want to maintain that energy level, it is critical to ensure that his energies are aimed in the right direction. The role you take on, or empower someone else to assume, in relation to this player is that of mentor.

4. A player who resists activities that lead to productivity, team interaction, and success, or who spreads rumors about others, serves as your terrorist behind the scenes and has to be dealt with immediately. This player typically has low levels of skill and/or asserts a low (and thus poor) attitude toward you, specifically, and management, in general. When you can mentally or physically plot a player into the lower left quadrant of the SA Model, the role you must assume is that of counselor.

What are some of the variables that lead players toward or away from any specific quadrant? Consider how the following environmental stimulants impact talent actions, feelings, and human-capital motivation: Merging organizations, business units, and teams; New positional requirements from a pre-existing person may put a person low on the vertical axis line and high on the horizontal axis line; Merging markets and competition; Decreased customer demand for specific products or services; Management changes (personnel or styles); Retiring peers or superiors; Fired peers or superiors; New product or service introductions in one of your markets; Increased organizational profits; Decreased organizational profits; Increased training and educational opportunities onsite; Decreased onsite educational and training opportunities; New transformer or high-performer talent introduced to the team; New player to the team turns out to be a negative catalyst; On-the-job traumas of some degree; Offsite traumas (in personal life, at home, with family members, and so on) to some degree.

Always remember that players are not static and will appear in differing SA Model management/player index quadrants.

Consider some of the explosive applications to this Managerial/Leadership/Coaching Engagement Model in your work environment today. Imagine you are sitting in a meeting and someone has said or done something to which you feel compelled to respond. Glancing down at your left hand, placed on your left kneecap, you visualize the SA Model with your finger pointing upward at a right angle to your thumb, and you score that person and situation against that gesture. Based upon the immediate situation and where that person is plotted, you now know which of the six managerial/leadership engagement styles is best for deployment.

In developing and managing Talent, the analytics of the L-Grid should align with the analytics of the Performance review. That is how the two models should calibrate on the top of the first page of the actual assessment instrument presented in this Chapter.

Another matrix many organizations use is a Tenure or Time-In-Grade/Position formula, and while these can be quantifiable and necessary for an individual to grasp and master the mechanics of a Position and the talent pool involved, these can sometimes be a source of derailment. You should consider an objective matrix by which, if an individual is accomplished in a Position, the organization does not penalize them for being efficient or even the Subject-Matter Expert in that area and hold them back from challenges and growth opportunities – i.e. promotion. In the marketplace today, true talent, pure talent, real talent will not bide their time waiting to be elevated or advanced within the talent pipeline. They will either decrease their commitment and input into the organization or they will look elsewhere for the opportunity to participate, shine and rise.

Remember, the overall employee experience is shaped and determined by how you (individually and organizationally) manage your side of each of the ACHIEVEMENT life cycle phases and what the individual employee receives, sees, observes, and internalizes as their EXPERIENCE along the way. Every touchpoint from the organization, whether intentional or unintentional, whether overt or not, still shapes the experience an individual has within the work environment.

A key aspect of TALENTification is the responsibility of every supervising manager primarily, and hiring manager secondarily, to be cognizant of what each person on their team does, what their growth goals are, what their growth potential is within that business unit or within the organization overall. Talent gaps, lacks and losses should be ata minimum if the ACHIEVEMENT process is at work. Learning of an impending employee departure because of employment growth opportunities with another employer, whether it is because the employee did not see themselves within your organization or because you failed to articulate your strategic plans for them, is a failure of the TALENTification succession process.

Individuals, likewise, should be aware of the TALENTification process, as well, and should feel comfortable communicating with their supervising manager, hiring manager and senior leaders about the goals/aspirations they have and whether they feel those are being met.

Business/C-Suite leaders at their respective levels must architect out their immediate, intermediate and long-term talent needs, growth migration patterns of personnel and the ongoing professional development needs in order for their business enterprise to survive and thrive – from both the technician skills/aptitudes requirements and professional KSAs -- to perform the TDR expected.

The degree of culture disruption, productivity disruption and profitability hits an organization takes annually due to these failures is massive and on a global basis. Architect out individual player aspirations for positional efficiency, productivity, profitability and development as it relates to the individual ... align this with succession needs.

In this part of the TALENTification process and the ACHIEVEMENT Model, the management and development of human capital is essential for sustained engagement, inclusion and profitability of the organization. Here too, AI influence and impact upon integrating, engaging, and effective talent inclusion will be critical for dynamic organizations, and with this will be the ever-emerging technology platforms to aid human resourcing in this endeavor. While AI can be a major force multiplier, there will be no replacement for the human commonsense meter: the analytics and the optics it provides are always database driven – good data analytics in, good analytics out and bad analytics in and misleading data out!

In considering any AI system, it should be a tool or resource that embodies the organization's Values, Vision and Mission Statement and allows for it to better address inclusion, culture and business needs in respect to talent development and talent management of both the present and long-term needs for the organization. TALENTification is about everything one does, and that an organization does, to be relevant. No AI approach should simply serve as a scorecard on which an organization is checking off the boxes of labor relations and governmental diversity balances at the expense of the actual organization's health.

Ideally, AI should accelerate KSA mapping of the individual with the present TDR, to be in alignment with the aspirations of both the employee/individual and their hiring manager and supervising manager. AI should also be able to map this against organizational needs, market expectations and succession life cycles.

One macro document that can be crafted between talent and leadership is the annual and career Performance Development Plan (PDP). As it should detail all of the immediate, intermediate and long-term Knowledge, Skills and Abilities (KSA) to perform now and future Tasks, Duties and Responsibilities (TDR); You can benchmark off of the *Player Capability Index®* formula for specifics to ensure that your PDP has real meaning, substantive Key Performance Indicators (KPI) – most PDPs are embarrassing from both a talent and leadership perspective in how vague, generic and meaningless they really are to the engagement of all parties and the continual development and evolution to your organizations most value resource – human capital!

Here is a PDP template we use with our clients, as designed from one of our best-in-industry clients:

Personal Development Plan/PDP

JeffreyMagee

Name _____

Goal (Results expected – what you will do to increase effectiveness)

Date _____

Competencies	Actions/Experiences	Resources	Target Dates	Measures of Achievement
Knowledge/Skills/Abilities (KSA): Specific skills or knowledge needed – What you want to develop or improve?	Methods of development – What actions you will take to develop these competencies?	Help with your development – What resources or people will support your learning?	(Dates and timelines for implementing the plan and follow-up actions)	Tasks, Duties, Responsibilities (TDR). What will success look like? How will I measure my progress? How will performance improve as a result of my development?

This instrument serves leadership and talent-in-question on multiple levels:

1. Management and Leadership can use this tool as a conversational and coaching instrument on a regular basis to ensure all parties involved are executing and progressing.

2. Management and Leadership can use this tool as a conversational and coaching instrument in regular official performance reviews.

3. Management and Leadership can use this tool as a conversational and coaching instrument in talent succession strategy sessions and discussions.

As you undertake this important Seventh phase of the ACHIEVE-MENT life cycle, always stay focused on how this applies to the TALENT in a multitude of applications. For an organization, it demands the understanding of each application and how they actually must align as one for ultimate ROI. Identify at each of the following five TALENT considerations, what you expect the new talent to do, TDR. This must be done first because it leads into the next crucial step: what KSAs are required to perform the role (TDR) you plan to put them in:

1. TALENT management of the INDIVIDUAL;

2. TALENT management of career PATHWAYS;

3. TALENT management of critical essential POSITION pathways;

4. TALENT management of secondary support POSITION pathways; and

5. TALENT management of the ORGANIZATION.

Understanding the life cycle of TALENTification is critical and we hope this book helps synthesize what we know about human capital and provides a simplified approach for individuals and organizations to move beyond the carousel of the past.

Dr. Jeffrey Magee

Chapter Eight

Move DEI(A) Talent Through
Succession

Move Talent Through Succession – A succession plan is essential to ensure the organization is thinking about the future – at every level and with every individual.

You should always be asking what is the *Flight Risk* of any key individual and every employee ultimately. Keeping in mind that Flight Risk is your dashboard view. Then compare this with what you know factual to be each key individual and ultimately every employee's *Intent-to-Stay*, these may be worlds apart!

There always should be internal Stay-Discussions, interviews and surveys to get valuable feedback on how you are executing on your DEI initiatives. Look for trends for who stays and who goes, and then why. What could have been done to engage and retain talent lost that you did not want to loose.

Ideally you want to have a succession plan for every supervisor role and higher, but from an organizational leadership perspective it's essential to identify the roles critical to the organization's success and to have a robust succession process for those roles. Ask yourself as you make these evaluations, what does the diversity and inclusion look like as you track from employee up through to the senior positions in your organization. Are we growing a diverse inclusion talent pool today and for tomorrow. As we move talent through our organizational journey map, does it reflect that we are as diverse as we need to be to be relevant? Are we as inclusive at every level as we should be? Are people of all diversity being equitably treated throughout the organization? Is this an organization that our people are advocates in their own sphere-of-influence when they are not at work?

In fact, part of an organization's fiduciary responsibility, and part of the Board of Directors' responsibility, is to review the succession plan annually. A key part of succession is linking it to the business strategy. The business strategy is future looking, and succession should be as well – where is the organization going and what kinds of talent will be needed to make sure the strategy succeeds? Succession runs hand-in-hand with development; by identifying internal talent for critical future roles you can focus development so the right person is ready for the right job at the right time.

Are we benchmarking our developmental plans against what individual employee's expectations are? How do we measure against others best-in-class in our industry and geography today?

Be aware of Micro Aggressions (verbal, environmental, behaviors, policies, actions, etc.) that can cause one to feel unwelcomed, not included, valued and underappreciated, work to eliminate and educate others to these as barriers to success.

KPIs: *Exploring how to promote and who is promotable from your five levels of Stars & Performers; Benchmark against your TALENT Horizon Report-Succession Development Span-of-Influence Chart; Etc.;*

Recently, I was sharing talent development and succession ideas with the Managing Partners (i.e. CEO/COO level individuals) of the top 100 largest CPA Firms in the world, which the AICPA had gathered and asked me to headline. The discussion came to succession plans and how many of them engage in this high-level client work – the response was in the upper 90 percentile. Then I polled the room on how frequently this work product is benchmarked and used in business development and talent discussion annually and the response plummeted to the low 20 percentile. Then I asked of these Managing Partners, how many of your Firms have succession and talent development plans – again high 90 percentile. And, you guessed it, when I polled that room on how often these are referenced – low teen percentile.

Interestingly, later that evening at a social reception a senior Partner to one of the global leading CPA Firm engaged me in discussion. He indicated that the program I presented was one of the most riveting he had experienced in years and provided significant new maps for consideration in their Firm and with their clients. But he indicated it really did not matter; at the end of the day, no one really cares about talent development or succession work. It is sexy and sounds good in the consultancy practice to clients, but they are making so much money off their clients that no one really cares about talent matters beyond having a document that someone can point to. But in terms of actually executing, it into a business on a 24/7 practice, no one cares – WOW!

Moving Talent through the Succession pipeline is a complex effort and one that cannot be set to the side as a once-a-year administrative paperwork activity and review.

Start with a simple organizational business model and gauge everything into and against that framework.

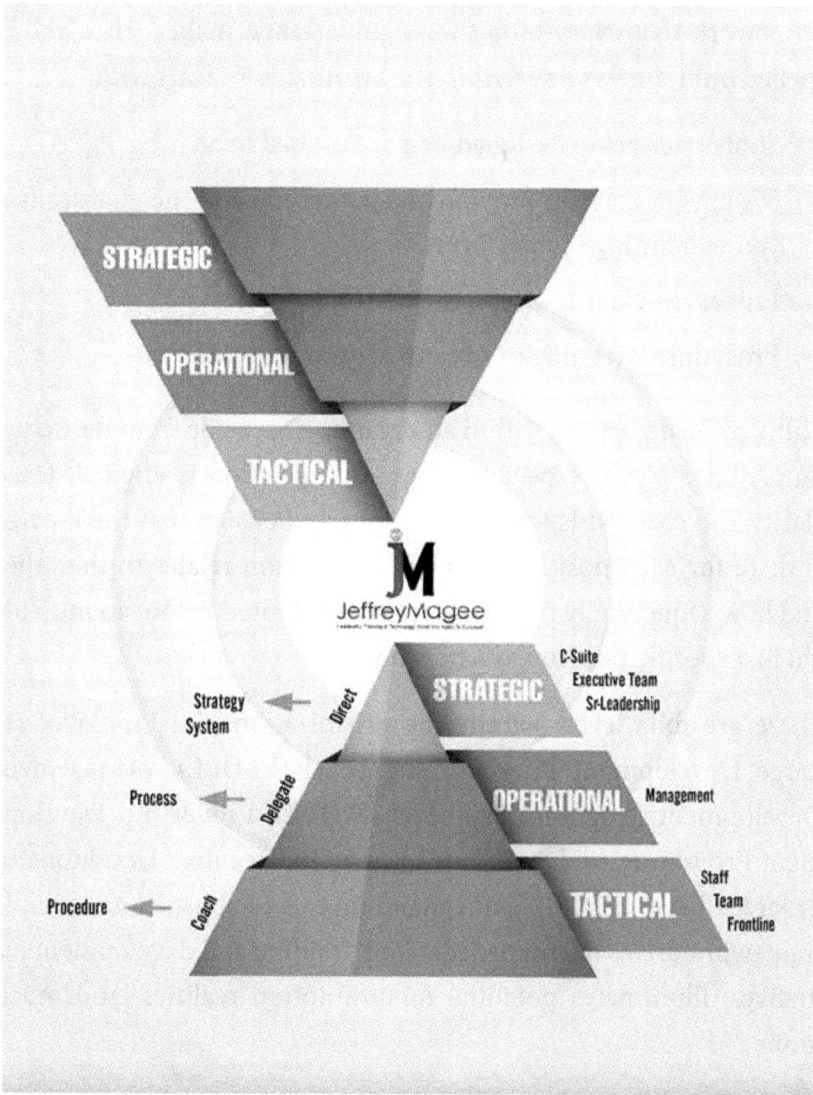

Not only does the business need to consider this diagram and what must be considered and accomplished from the top downward, it must also ensure that with each persona and that within the DEI framework that everything that is undertaken makes since and is spelled out for everyone within the organization. Start with:

- Strategy clearing designed and articulated to all
- Systems in place to provide understanding and the guardrails if you will for how to perform
- Process in place to ensure successful activities
- Procedures to guide minimum actions of excellence

Think of each position within an organization, aside from the actual human capital, in respect to where that position is aligned. Have clarity and clear KPIs for each position and ensure that the linkage is there for each position in how one position relates to the other and how sequentially positions must be executed before an individual in a specific position ascends upward.

There are four levels within any organization. the Employee-at-Large Development Programming Level (ELDPL), Management Development Programming Level (MDPL), Leadership Development Programming Level (LDPL) and the Executive Development Program Level (EDPL). Understanding this established and simple framework drives talent management, training and development initiatives, illuminates potential for promotion realities, and much more.

As positions and individuals ascend into the Executive ranks or the Executive Development Programming Levels (EDPL), the focus and commitments for moving talent through succession model reverses.

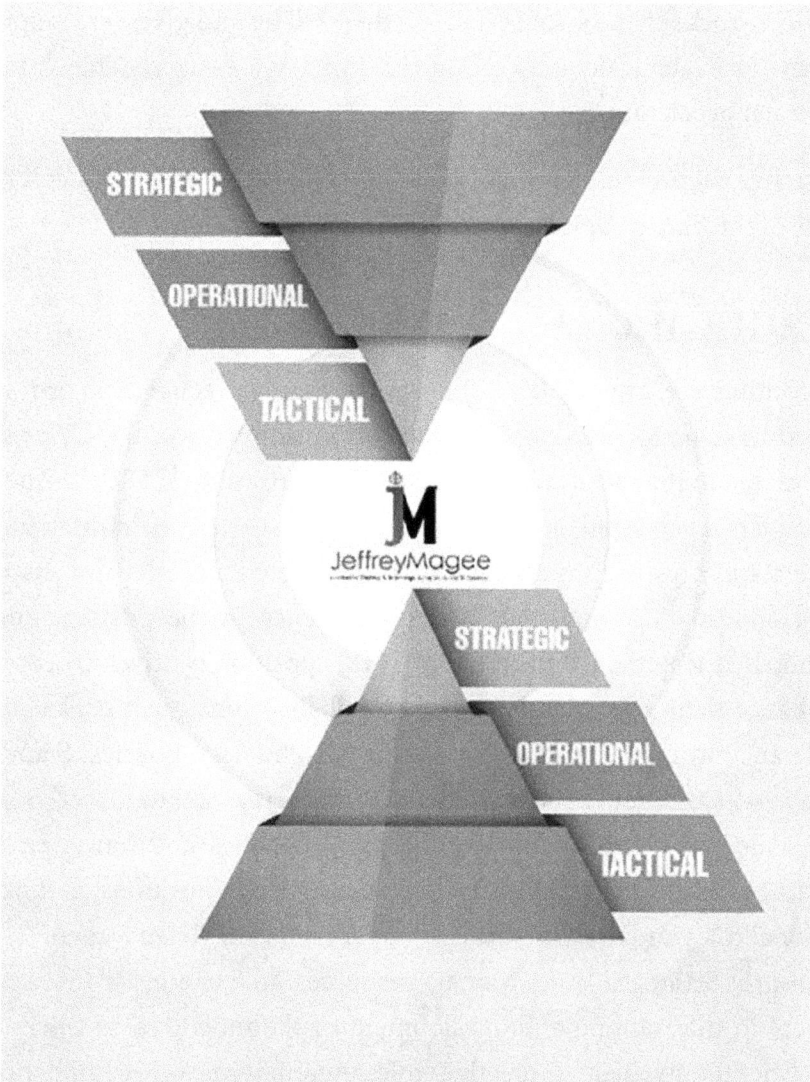

STRATEGIC

OPERATIONAL

TACTICAL

JM

JeffreyMagee

STRATEGIC

OPERATIONAL

TACTICAL

Let's examine this visually through the *Talent Development Pyramid* model we use to move talent through a succession model.

As stated, think of your Succession Plan document(s) as a human-capital road map. It foresees where every turn, bump, curve, cliff, falling rock, or instance of bad weather will be and gives you ample time to strategically plan around and through every roadblock for greater accelerated success.

Each position is clearly associated to one of these three distinct levels of the *Talent Development Pyramid* model:

TACTICAL Level:

Frontline *employees and positions* must simply execute a job or role and must be focused upon the execution simplicity of the KPIs associated to that position's Task-Duty-Responsibility (TDR); The position must calibrate the employee (occupant to that position) to understand how best to execute that role, know the TDRs and shape all endeavors around supporting excellence in the position and thereby the person within that role; This position is driven by compliance mentality, mandates and compliance constituents (aka adherence to organizational Employee Handbook & Policies, Standards-of-Conduct, Safety Guidelines, Industry Standards & Best Practices, Governmental Regulatory Guidelines and Laws, etc.); Most typical organizations would identify these positions as functional roles and first line "leads," "supervisors," or "team leaders" …; Disproportionate time, money, resources and energy is invested here in the training and development of the individual to operate efficiently in their respective role. Again, typically compliance driven and a lesser degree of professional talent development endeavors take place here.

OPERATONAL Level:

Progressing or ascending upward from TACTICAL Position level would be the individuals that have demonstrated performance excellence and understanding of the TACTICAL level. Now, these *employees and positions* progress beyond, yet must still maintain the TACICAL understanding of the tactical simplicity of the ability to execute a job or role of the KPIs associated to that positions Task-Duty-Responsibility (TDR); This position at the OPERATIONAL level must calibrate the employee (occupant to that position) to understand how best not just to execute that role, but they must now have an understanding of planning, seeing the bigger macro perspective and increased responsibilities are assigned and greater level of performance is expected; Here the position demands the occupant have the ability to understand the Who, What, When, Where, Why and How to each position and how they inter relate to others organizationally; Understanding the TDRs and shape all endeavors around supporting excellence in the position and thereby the person within that role; This position is driven by compliance mentality, mandates and compliance constituents (aka adherence to organizational Employee Handbook & Policies, Standards-of-Conduct, Safety Guidelines, Industry Standards & Best Practices, Governmental Regulatory Guidelines and Laws, etc.); At this positional level participation in designing these KPIs take place, it is more than just execution at this second level within the ***Talent Development Pyramid*** model. Most typical organizations would identify these positions as second line leaders like, "managers" or "junior leadership" ... Here, we start to see of percentage migration away from a disproportionate time, money, resources and energy is invested here in the training and development of the individual to operate efficiently in their respective role, again with a descending percentage of time, money and resources on the compliance side of professional talent development endeavors and now a beginning increase on the professional people or talent skill development taking place.

STRATEGIC Level:

Progressing or ascending upward from the TACTICAL Position level through the OPERATIONAL Position level and into the STRATEGIC Position level, would once again be the individuals that have demonstrated performance excellence and understanding of the TACTICAL and OPERATIONAL levels ideally, but not necessarily always a requirement. At this level, the ability to execute a job or role of the KPIs associated to that positions Task-Duty-Responsibility (TDR) is elevated to a more macro level. This position at the STRATEGIC level must calibrate the employee (occupant to that position) to understand how values and vision drive the organizational health; This position is driven by more than a compliance mentality, mandates and compliance constituents (aka adherence to organizational Employee Handbook & Policies, Standards-of-Conduct, Safety Guidelines, Industry Standards & Best Practices, Governmental Regulatory Guidelines and Laws, etc.), at this level the position requires the occupant be the architect of these policies, documents and drivers of the organizations' *Talent Development Pyramid* model; Most typical organizations would identify these positions as second line leaders like, "directors," "Vice presidents," "senior-leadership," "executive suite" or members of the "C-Suite" ... Here we see a minimal technician level of time, money, resources and energy invested in the training and development of the individual to operate efficiently in their respective role, and the necessity for a significant increase of time, money and resources in professional people or talent skill development.

As individuals evolve into this third level of the *Talent Development Pyramid* model, it becomes inverted and now opens a new set of realities that are expected of the senior leader. At this level, each Position demands that a new and set of Tasks, Duties and Responsibilities (TDR) be singled out for each Position/Role and a clear pathway is mapped out for each individual. There will become a new inverted *Talent Development Pyramid* model that addresses a new level of TACTICAL, OPERATIONAL and STRATEGIC Knowledge, Skills and Abilities (KSA) that one must possess or that the organization must craft out for development of the new individuals success pathway.

To ensure an organization is healthy and operational for its key stakeholders, it is essential that each person -- no matter what their capacity or level of DEI participation is within the organization or at what level of operation one may be -- that a succession development pathway be created with their consideration. It should map out where a person and position are, and what the necessary developmental and experiential growth needs are to be relevant at that level and to calibrate one to be functionable for promotion to any next horizontal or vertical level.

<u>Consider these essential questions at the outset, if you do not have a Succession Plan.</u>

1. What happens if the senior-most leader is no longer here?
2. What happens if any key business-unit leader is no longer here?

3. What happens if every key business-unit leader is no longer here?

4. What happens if the most-seasoned member of the team is no longer here?

5. What happens if the most valuable member to the organization, in your estimation, is no longer here?

6. If you have any outsourced personnel necessary to function, what happens if they are no longer here? Or the outsourced organization supplying staff is no longer here?

7. What do you do to engage, develop, manage and track the talent progression of your most valuable new hire?

8. What do you do to engage, develop, manage and track the talent progression of every new hire?

9. What do you do to engage, develop, manage and track the talent progression of every employee at every level within your organization?

10. What do you do to plot the positions necessary, within your organization, and the sequencing of one to another?

11. What do you do to ensure you keep great talent?

12. What do you do to ensure you are engaging and developing your talent horizontally within your organization to grow their mental DNA and keep them engaged in the organization when you can't elevate upwards vertically by promotion at any given time?

13. What do you do to elevate and promote individuals based upon performance and value to the organization, regardless of tenure, to ensure you keep that talent pool and maintain an upward flow of talent without resulting in a bottleneck of talent at the mid-

level positions, due to no movement at the upper levels. The Up-and-Out movement of talent should be based upon performance and value to an organization and not based upon who lives the longest within your organization – tenure alone as the qualifier for promotion is the death knell to organizations of the future!

Now, considering these eleven essential questions, when examining your Succession Plan, does the strategic and tactical intent spelled out address these questions?

To grow your organization-wide Talent, the senior leaders should drive the discussion, focusing on the critical positions within the organization necessary to survive and thrive. Then, look at the human capital that you have to populate those positions and which positions are vacant. Determine if you are, in fact, in need of new great talent. This determination then serves as the initial framework for driving Succession conversations. The key Talent development professionals within the organization own this enterprise. These conversations can then be used as the framework for more micro discussions with each hiring and supervising manager, in order to detail out their sphere-of-influence Talent conversations.

The Talent conversation can include:

1. Educational development needs by position and individual;

2. Technician-level needs that an individual must possess to perform core functionality of position;

3. Immediate, intermediate and long-term PDP plans that address the TDAs needed;

4. Realistic date lines for KPI accomplishments and advancements;

5. Timelines to develop existing Talent in their current roles and establish success pathways for their movement;

6. What core experiences are essential for an individual to grasp, perfect and demonstrate competency within to ascend to the next horizontal or vertical position;

7. If you need to engage in an outreach effort to find new Talent, onboard them and get them into fundamental operational levels. What would that look like and what timelines would need to be considered.

8. As you move any one individual through the talent process, you must now measure their desire to grow and move. As they do, calculate your bench strength for who next ascends and are you developing them accordingly, so when one person moves up, their position is smoothly and competently backfilled.

These questions, and others organic to your unique environment, will then place accountability on the organization's human resources and senior leadership to ensure that the resources, financials, staffing, etc., are allocated to address all of this movement.

As you consider and schedule the movement of talent through the succession evolution process, ensure considerations for inhouse and off-site professional development and educational training needs, whether formal or informal, technical or on-technical, certification or non-certification leveled. Make sure that you budget time and financial resources for these endeavors, and that you have the talent resources to backfill any temporary assignments that may take an individual out of play for any period of time.

Also, a critical consideration, what succession movement compliance issues are required that can enhance or derail your talent needs, and thus, organization efficiencies? One client organization I worked with had required training courses for advancement of individuals. They had a bottleneck of mid-level personnel not being promoted because individuals were unable to attend this theory-based training program/course/schooling. Everyone was actually involved with the crisis in real time. This continued for several years until someone dared to ask why. This issue was immediately resolved, massive promotions took place, and the unobservant faculty and leaders of this institutionalized theory-based training program/course/schooling were removed to keep from imploding the talent pipeline further.

Remember, the overall employee experience is shaped and determined by how you (individually and organizationally) manage your side of each of the ACHIEVEMENT life cycle phases and what the individual employee receives, sees, observes, and internalizes as their EXPERIENCE along the way. Every touchpoint from the organization, whether intentional or unintentional, whether overt or not, still shapes the experience an individual has within the work environment.

Moving talent through the organization, should be based upon more than tenure; which in many organizations is exactly how this arcane asinine process has been and is administered. Knowledge transfer is essential for peak performance of an organization, and an objective matrix for determining how and when to evaluate individuals for promotion is critical.

Utilizing your "Performance Review & Development Assessment" (like the one presented in Chapter Seven as a template) can provide analytics for objectively evaluating and sequencing promotions of your talent force. Another model that serves as a baseline within the human resource industry, is the *Figure 7.3 SA Model* presented within the previous Chapter and using that base score as an overlay to "Potential for Promotion." This can become a very subjective, political conversation in organizations unless one has a matrix that can be applied.

To identify where your current talent stars are and where tomorrow's talent stars may be, consider "Potential for Promotion" along a similar L-Grid model. Individuals within the bottom left tw quadrants of the *Figure 7.3 SA Model,* are not only not worthy of being on your dashboard of considerations for promotability, the conversations and strategic focus must be on dramatic wake-up calls for those in jeopardy of immediate removal from your organization, for all of the reasons provided in previous Chapters. When management fails at either, the senior leader's conversations and strategic focus must pick up where management left off.

Managerial-Leadership-Coaching Engagement Model

This model looks at your ability and attitude, and from that it determines whether you're in need of a coach, mentor, counselor, manager, disciplinarian, or teacher. Please rank yourself using values of 1-10 on both your ability and your attitude. The graph will automatically plot the points. The person who is currently your manager you will rank you as well.

	Attitude	Ability
My Perspective	9	8
Manager's Perspective	6	5

Engagement Model

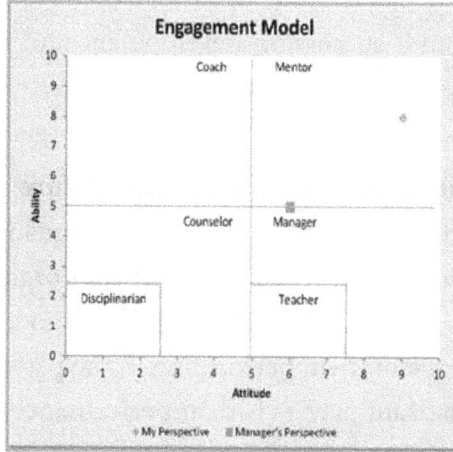

When you consider individuals with potential for promotion, it is a reflection upon how they presently and consistently execute their Job Performance, the analytics of their Job Description and how well they demonstrate the attitudinal fiber from acceptable to rock stardom. The higher one's scores are on both the vertical axis and horizontal axis of the *Figure 7.3 SA Model*, the greater the potential is for promotability.

Your human-capital talent are "**STARS.**" There are five core sets of Talent Stars in an organization and where each individual land within the "Potential for Promotion" correlate to this L-Grid model.

1. **Superstars/Peak Performers** - Your top talent always lands in the upper right most quadrant (block) and these are your "Superstars." These individuals demonstrate the ability to execute and a desire for continuous learning and development. It takes additional attention of talent-management professionals, their

immediate supervising managers and senior leaders to recognize ways to keep them engaged, provide them with appropriately challenging work and opportunities. Equally important, from a succession development and retention point, what are the realities in relation to each player in this quadrant to retain and grow them for their and the organization's future.

2. **Future Stars/Evolving Stars/Future Performers** -Those individuals landing in the upper left quadrant (block) are your potential "Future Stars" within your organization. These individuals possess the KSAs to perform and, most likely, there is evidence of them performing in the past. The reality of the top left quadrant players is their performance issues center around attitudinal, work-ethic, passion, motivation, and self-esteem variables and that is where the talent-engagement conversations must focus. With corrective engagement, these individuals can adjust their performance the quickest and transition from top left to top right quadrant placement the fastest, and thus, can be potential future "Superstars" within your organization.

3. **Developing Stars/Developing Performers** – The bottom right quadrant (block) is where you find your "Developing Stars," as they need appropriately sequenced educational and training exposure, as well as OTJ TDR growth. As their knowledge and performance improves, ideally they would graduate upward to the top right quadrant of the assessment model and become your "Superstars" of tomorrow.

4. **Falling Stars/Crashing Stars/Non-Performers** – These individuals consume far too much mental time of others and impact the culture, climate, and talent effectiveness of the entire team or organization in an adverse manner. These are the individuals

who land in the bottom left quadrant (block) of the L-Grid and are your "Falling/Crashing Stars". If we are to assume that the organization did not just hire an individual that scored low on both the vertical axis of the L-Grid (KSA) and low on the horizontal axis of the L-Grid (poor to toxic attitudes), these individuals must have backslid due to identifiable factors. These factors can be documented, addressed, and corrective talent-development actions must take place immediately or begin to take steps to remove them from your team/organization as quickly as possible.

As your organization evolves through the talent process, note that organizations that build their immediate business portfolios around their "Superstars" sustain business for today. Organizations that build their business portfolios around their "Future Stars" sustain business for tomorrow. Organizations that build their business portfolios around their "Developing Stars" will have business for the future. And, organizations that do not address their "Falling/Crashing Stars" will be fortunate to be in business over the long term.

There is one more category of your Talent Stars for consideration in ensuring all talent is actively on your radar

5. Unknown Stars/Unknown Performers - This would be the demographic within every organization that the talent professionals and leaders may not really know at any level, the "Unknown Star." The larger an organization becomes, the greater the likelihood becomes that there are individuals that you don't really see on your L-Grid. These are the individuals on your payroll ledger, yet you look at their "name" and realize you do not know them

very well or at all. This is where you must identify how you and they fell out of the ACHIEVEMENT process.

To enhance your ability to identify where your current talent stars are and where tomorrow's talent stars may be, consider "Potential for Promotion" along a similar L-Grid model. Individuals within the bottom left two quadrant of the *Figure 7.3 SA Model*, are not only not worthy of being on your dashboard of considerations for promotability, the conversations and strategic focus must be on dramatic wake-up calls, for all of the reasons provided in previous Chapters. Make sure you know where your "STARS" are at all times.

A key aspect of TALENTification is the responsibility of every supervising manager primarily, and hiring manager secondarily, to be cognizant of what each person on their team does, what their growth goals are, what their growth potential is within that business unit or within the organization overall. Talent gaps, lacks and losses should be ata minimum if the ACHIEVEMENT process is at work. Learning of an impending employee departure because of employment growth opportunities with another employer, whether it is because the employee did not see themselves within your organization or because you failed to articulate your strategic plans for them, is a failure of the TALENTification succession process.

Individuals, likewise, should be aware of the TALENTification process, as well, and should feel comfortable communicating with their supervising manager, hiring manager and senior leaders about the goals/aspirations they have and whether they feel those are being met.

Business/C-Suite leaders at their respective levels must architect out their immediate, intermediate and long-term talent needs, growth migration patterns of personnel and the ongoing professional development needs in order for their business enterprise to survive and thrive – from both the technician skills/aptitudes requirements and professional KSAs -- to perform the TDR expected.

The degree of culture disruption, productivity disruption and profitability hits an organization takes annually due to these failures is massive and on a global basis. Architect out individual player aspirations for positional efficiency, productivity, profitability and development as it relates to the individual ... align this with succession needs.

When it comes to moving through the talent pipeline, each person has their own timeline of expectations for experience gained, opportunity experienced, compensation growth and potential rank/title ascension. It is critical that leadership always be mindful of this, especially in respect to rising talent stars and the stars in which the organizational enterprise has invested significant time/resources/money in grooming. It is asinine for an organization to grow its talent base and allow itself to easily lose such vested stakeholders, merely to appease the ego of individuals in the C-Suite!

Here is where you direct your attention and initiatives at every managerial-leadership level, along with the HR Team and C-Suite at the horizon opportunities in your organization, as it relates to human capital – talent.

At this level, there should be a master human capital talent tracking system in place that illustrates where your talent is and needs are, as it relates to succession management. Each managerial-supervisory level player (MDP) that rates/scores/assesses their direct reports, should be the front line in completing the following diagram. It should be presented and defended up-line to the leadership team (LDP), and ultimately senior most leaders/executives (EDP) should be aware of and have an understanding of where their strengths, weaknesses, opportunities, threats and critical gaps/lapses in adequate human capital and engagement.

This *Horizon Report: TALENT Succession Development Span-of-Control™ Chart* is essential in hiring, developing, promoting, retaining your talent.

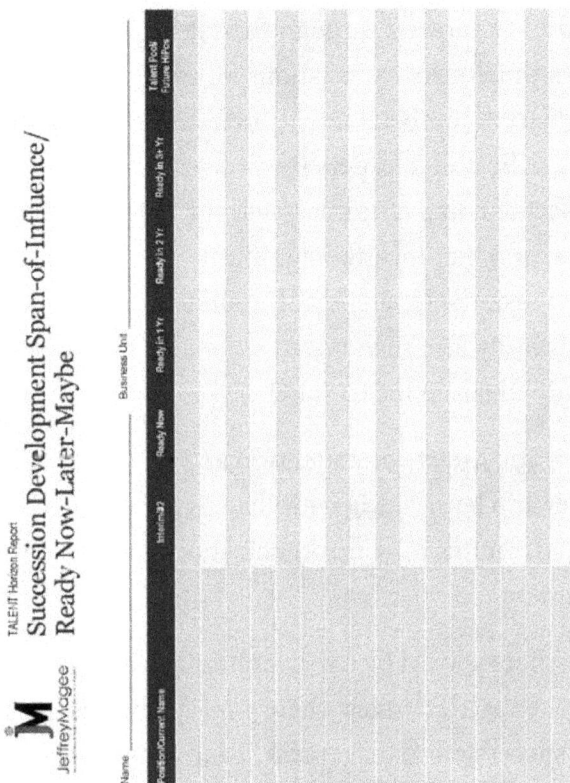

This ***Horizon Report: TALENT Succession Development Span-of-Control™ Chart*** allows leaders and organizations to strategically identify critical talent in positions within an organization by "Name" and "Position," so as to evaluate based upon performance reviews, accomplishments, anecdotal evidence, evaluating one through the lens of the Player Capability Index Model and measured KPIs of their potential for promotability. At the same time, it serves as an accountability tool for managers, leaders and executives to ensure talent management of multiple strategic questions and talent management succession considerations:

1. If that identified critical player were promoted or unavailable for any reason who could or would be the "Interim #2" player in that Position?

2. Who is actually "Ready Now" to assume that critical initial Position? And in many instances in many organizations the pipeline of talent is very questionable only one-level deep?

3. Then you can start evaluating how you are engaging others and developing others in both any one business area or across horizontal business lines of human capital development opportunities and ensuring that the ACHIEVEMENT process is alive and robustly being implemented. Now, you can start evaluating how managers and leaders are developing their respective teams and benches as they say, who would be ready for advancement in the next "1-Year, 2-Years, 3-Years, etc." …

This is an essential observation, as employees that believe they are ready for advancement and are not getting said opportunities will start to mentally check-out on you and will become receptive to outside opportunities and you may never realize this until they day they say *good-bye*!

This ***Horizon Report: TALENT Succession Development Span-of-Control™ Chart*** is essential in holding you accountable and in holding everyone in the organization accountable to the ACHIEVEMENT process and in developing and retaining your human capital talent.

If you were to evaluate your **Present-State** and look at where your human capital lands in the diagram, then look at it through the lens of DEI and see if you have inherent biases that you did not were present, yet become glaring when you see where your people land at each position across your organization and within each vertical layer from bottom to top?

This can guide your actions, strategies and awareness in building a string **Future-State** of your organization and you own mindset!

As you undertake this important Eighth phase of the ACHIEVEMENT life cycle, always stay focused on how this applies to the TALENT throughout other applications. For an organization, it demands the understanding of each application and how they actually must align as one for ultimate ROI. Identify at each of the following five TALENT considerations what you expect the new talent to do, i.e., TDR. This must be done first because it leads into the next crucial step: what KSAs are required to perform the role (TDR) you plan to put them in:

1. TALENT management of the INDIVIDUAL;

2. TALENT management of career PATHWAYS;

3. TALENT management of critical essential POSITION pathways;

4. TALENT management of secondary support POSITION pathways; and

5. TALENT management of the ORGANIZATION.

Understanding the life cycle of TALENTification is critical and we hope this book helps synthesize what we know about human capital while providing a simplified approach for individuals and organizations to move beyond the carousel of the past.

Chapter Nine

Evaluate Your DEI(A) Model Or Process –

Evaluate Your Model or Process – DEI should be about open pathways for everyone and then 100 percent true merit based upon quantifiable data, not personal opinions, from the frontline to the executive room. This is the data analysis phase, and built off of the data collected at each previous level in the ACHIEVEMENT Model. Along with any established data collection KPIs you track, also consider data around: Trends in business, Risk Management items, Customer needs and satisfaction, Customer experiences with you, Supply chain, Compliance, DEI, People performance, etc. Create transparent dashboards of data that you want people to see, to drive DEI goals into actuality.

All next steps aligned with previous KPIs: *Planning; Forecasting of Human-Capital Needs against Positions, Creating of WPxF=ROI formulas, Organizational, Market, Growth, P&L, Individual Needs/Aspirations/Goals; Attrition Management needs, etc.; How does this integrate into Business Plans, Mission Statements and Values; Benchmark against your talent audits by individual, business unit needs and organizational strategic planning, 3-Deep Mindset; Radical Relevance/RE5 Modeling applied here; Etc.*

Global Fortune 100 Firms are committed to DEI within their organizations and in many instances with the vendors they do work with. The same I find with my work with proactive, future focused Generals within the United States Military, and both institutions share one critical factor in common, which has led to their perpetual success for the last one-hundred years. When adhered to, it ensured success and when dismissed, almost assuredly crises and derailments appear. The ability to evaluate in real time, and afterward, as a lesson learned; either way, critical After-Action Reviews of your talent process can generate greater levels of ROI.

This important Ninth phase of the ACHIEVEMENT process only fixates upon real-time, daily fluency KPIs. This is critical for DEI with the executive and ownership team, leaders and to hold Employee Resource Groups/Employee Engagement Groups equally accountable – identify and use your scorecards before-during-after regularly.

Calibrate your talent-management processes to include After-Action Review opportunities. These can be facilitated by hiring managers, supervising managers or human resource managers. They can continuously solicit feedback from appropriate individuals who will provide you with feedback on individual progress, growth and effectiveness of talent and talent leadership. This could be incorporated in the 30-, 60-, 90-, or 120-day onboarding process discussed earlier in this book; it could be a consultative piece of any leader-to-leader discussions on talent; and it could be incorporated into team peer reviews, performance reviews, promotion discussions, etc.

The Five simple steps to an After-Action Review conversation or document focus a healthy conversation around:

1. Review what was supposed to take place by the initial or original action plan;

2. Review what actually did take place;

3. What went right from your take away and implemented strategies/ops/actions;

4. What did not work out as expected; and

5. What did you learn and what can be calibrated for continued accelerated success/ROI?

Always be evaluating, not as an attempt to throw anyone under the bus, but as Jim Collins made infamous in his leadership book, *GOOD TO GREAT*, the bus metaphor is your organization, team, business unit, etc., and great is dependent upon having only the right people on your bus. Get people into the correct positions on the bus, and those left over must be removed from your bus. The real-time analytics of how your talent process is performing and how your human capital is performing, is really critical for immediate success and early stage recalibration for potential gaps, cracks, and problems.

Your Business Plan or Strategic Intent will serve as a great reference point both in real-time and as a strategic calibrator to where your talent life cycle must be and how it should be performing at any time for organizational effectiveness. If you find that individual areas within a business are not performing to standards or exceeding standards, you have a human-capital talent issue. This must be addressed in real time -- immediately -- as the longer it goes on unaddressed, the more time the cascading negative ramifications has to spread throughout your organization, which can have years of residual fallout!

The importance of the Ninth element can't be overstated. So many organizations invest time, energy and money into creating a business community or diversity plan and in designing what they believe is a fluid talent identification, management, development and succession process, only to have massive human-capital turnover, disruptions in efficiencies and systemic failures – it's no wonder, when you forget this stage and/or fail to execute this stage.

Your intent of TALENTification, regardless of whether you hang the DEI name-sign onto it is simple. DIVERSITY should always be attracted diversity of human capital that shares an aligned VALUE and this allows for maximum alignments of:

- Thoughts
- Experiences
- Wisdom
- Innovation
- Collaboration
- Networks and Networking

- Goals
- Community
- Support
- Caring
- Celebration

However, if you are in an organization that pays a great deal of lip-service to this topic and many others, while actually systematically ensuring the opposite, you will never truly attain greatness, nor will you ever keep your best talent.

One government military agency, which has a great deal of influence over one of my clients, invests roughly $100,000.00 in one talent position every year. Every year for the past two decades, it onboards nearly a thousand new individuals and every year hundreds fail to achieve ROI and remain. Imagine the ability to have a failure of millions of dollars annually just in human-capital compensation packages, not to mention the residual financial and institutional losses.

This is a classic case study of failure in every phase of the ACHIEVE-MENT process about which you have been reading, and most critically, a failure at this Ninth level. Even with massive quantifiable data on the KPI failures, it is solely "ego" that perpetuates this. Good thing, in this case, we are discussing a government agency wherein financial failure is never a problem and is acceptable by the senior leaders of that organization.

So the question is, how can such massive failure be acceptable? Easy answer. The talent process in question has become one of a compliance role, rather than a functionality. We are provided with a checklist to show that each step was addressed; however, what is not addressed is the competence of the talent pool in question to execute and the talent management/development personnel to be able to actually perform their role. So real-time evaluation of Process and Models does not take place. What does take place is an institutionalization of ineffective processes and models.

This same case study holds true in any business that creates initiatives, processes, procedures, programs, etc., which once launched, merely places everyone in administrative or delivery mode and no one asks:

1. If what is being done really matters;
2. Are we generating the ROI we started out to gain;
3. Is what we do in alignment with what you state your Values, Vision and Mission to be;
4. Is what we do sustainable;
5. Are you capturing the human capital of our organization at its best to be its best;
6. Are you developing talent at each level for growth and sustainability, etc.

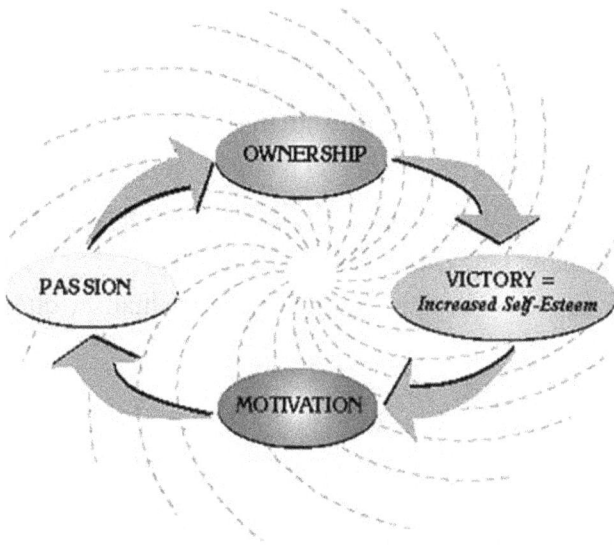

It's faster to evaluate talent success in the execution phase. In working with Anheuser-Busch and Pfizer Pharmaceuticals, I worked with their talent leadership to identify the optics around creating an engaged workforce. We learned a simple four-element model to creating an environment and culture for fully engaged talent success, identifying how to set human capital up for success and wins ASAP, and then get out of their way.

In evaluating your processes and talent management models in real time for optimal performance, you can identify a quantity of KPIs for each of the four elements by doing reverse analysis to determine where talent management's first obligation lies.

Let's consider two questions at each level, it is always the same two questions to get to the talent management baseline for understanding TALANTification. Not only is this helpful, here, at the Ninth phase of the ACHIEVEMENT process, but you can also apply this model as an accelerator at every phase of the ACHIEVEMENT process. If creating an organization wherein we have individuals who freely assume OWNERSHIP of their roles (Job Description), that generates some interesting analytics. What we recognize at work and at home, is the more you fixate on getting talent to assume Ownership of their life, responsibilities, job, endeavors, etc., the harder it actually becomes and the greater the level of talent derailments become. So here are the real-time evaluation questions for consideration:

Question One – When you get to do the things that you like to do or associate with the people that you like to associate with, does that create Passion or take away Passion?

Obvious answer – it creates Passion. So, what we learned is that OWNERSHIP is a byproduct of Passion and when you can create an environment wherein talent is passionate about what they do and who they get to engage, and you know the KPIs to feeding that Passion, you get greater levels of engagement and Ownership.

Therefore, OWNERSHIP is a byproduct of Passion. The more you concentrate talent endeavors to speak to Passion, the more you will experience organizations with greater levels of engaged mental and physical talent.

> *Question Two* – *When you get to do the things that you are Passionate about or associate with the people that you are Passionate about, does that create Motivation or take away Motivation?*

Obvious answer – it creates Motivation. So, what we learned next is that OWNERSHIP is a byproduct of Passion and Passion is a byproduct of Motivation. When you can create an environment wherein talent is Motivated about what they do and you know the

KPIs to feeding individuals and group Motivation, you get greater levels of engagement and Ownership.

Therefore, PASSION is a byproduct of Motivation. The more you concentrate talent endeavors to speak to Motivation, the more you will experience organizations with greater levels of Passion that will generate greater levels of engaged mental and physical talent, with greater levels of Ownership taking place.

> *Question Three – So then we took this a step further.... And here is where we discovered another layer to the TALENTification process ... When you know what you are good at doing, because you have done it and/or observed it, and are given an opportunity to perform and succeed, what happens to your self-esteem and psychology when you achieve success or have a Victory?*

Obvious answer – VICTORY feeds and creates Motivation. Motivation feeds and creates Passions. Passion feeds and creates a hunger, a desire, an addiction to assume OWNERSHIP of that which we do or associate with that affords us our next VICTORY; and now, with a development Talent organization, you can see greater achievement in real time from everything that you and others do!

A key piece of the entire ACHIEVEMENT talent process is to create pathways for greater successes for everyone, as often as possible and in the most efficient manner possible. Now once an individual has mastered consecutive, repeated success and has ongoing VICTORIES, talent leadership owns ensuring that complacency does not creep in and that individuals are continuously growing. It will be your real-time measurements that illuminate where individuals are and what your next steps shall be.

Throughout the talent life-cycle you may also be using Performance Assessment and other social-style or personality-style modeling instruments. Benchmark this data on a regular basis (maybe monthly coaching check-in sessions with talent-development personnel) with individuals to ensure that they are monitoring their efforts and interactions with their sphere of interactivity and are, in fact, generating desired and needed ROI. Make sure any launch data for a new Position or Project incorporates detailed KPIs that can provide real-time assessment for effectiveness and efficiencies.

You can also use peer feedback and client feedback from interactions or from engagement in projects with one another for evaluation.

Administratively review the organization to ensure talent is not being delayed opportunities for growth or promotion, due to a small group or individual being the sole gatekeeper to forward momentum, assignments, promotions, retention and terminations. I had a major global organization, at a regional level, losing massive talent out of their system and not understanding why. After some observations and interviews, what became apparent was that the senior-most leaders had placed far too much trust, authority and confidence in one person. This person was running the enterprise as their own fiefdom: those who were his buddies were coddled, promoted and given the best opportunities, at the expense of junior talent weighing the options of remaining and biding time or exploring new, and in many cases, better opportunities elsewhere. Sadly, the organization decided to do nothing and wait until the key gatekeeper retired instead of addressing it immediately. This, in turn, created more bad ill will throughout the organization and loss of desire for involvement at a peak-talent performer level.

Remember, the overall employee experience is shaped and determined by how you (individually and organizationally) manage your side of each of the ACHIEVEMENT life cycle phases and what the individual employee receives, sees, observes, and internalizes as their EXPERIENCE along the way. Every touchpoint from the organization, whether intentional or unintentional, whether overt or not, still shapes the experience an individual has within the work environment.

In evaluating your process and talent models, always be asking the disruptive questions that others would feel are off limits, Ask questions to discover if you are the best and how you know that there aren't even greater levels of ACHIEVEMENT that can be attained at every level and by every person. The new reality of human-resource capital is to evaluate every variable, and every talent pipeline touchpoint and recognize that what ensures talent growth is a never-ending attitude and hunger for achieving, winning and driving forward, coupled with an intensive never-ending approach at every level for professional development and training.

Likewise, in evaluating your process, procedures and systems, benchmark against your talent audits by positional needs and individuals, as discussed in Chapter two. Also benchmark against talent audits across business-unit needs and organizational strategic-planning objectives.

Design or access industry talent audits of what KSAs are the minimum required for every functioning position, job, task, duty in your organization. If there are gaps in the data analytics, pull together your super achievers in each role or position for their insights in creating your audit inventory. You can approach your talent-audit templates as if you were creating a "certification" process for each position, duty or task. Ask and answer what would be the minimum KSAs you would set as minimums and maximums for each. This can give you baselines for performance.

From a macro perspective, undertake annual talent audits across your organization to provide you analytics and forecasting abilities addressing the TALENTification Model. Apply the simple 5W and 1H formula to your talent discussions. As an example:

1. *What* do our talent audits reveal we possess right now across our headcount?

2. *Who* are our super achievers, achievers, and underachievers right now and what are our engagement plans for each?

3. *Where* is our talent now and where do they want to transition to positionally (organizationally, geographically, etc.) and *when* do they expect movement -- in the next year, two years, five years, etc.?

4. On an individual basis, what are their *whys* and why do they hold that position or view?

5. *How* do they expect to get from where they are to where they want to be?

You can also break this exercise down by

1. Staff Level,

2. Management Level,

3. Leadership Level, and

4. Executive Level

Then, from this exercise, you can consider for each level of personnel analysis, within your organization or down at the frontline business unit level, how talent may be impacted. These results will determine how your TALENTification Process needs to be geared to address and respond to the

1. Recruitment Phase (Hire or Re-Hire);

2. Retention Phase;

3. Development Phase;

4. Promotion/Transition/HR Alignment Phases;

5. Growth Phase (as a business); and the

6. Attrition Phase (departures, termination, retirement, burn-out, etc.).

While an organization can have great strategic plans and in-depth talent capabilities, they need to always be calibrated annually (if not on a more regular basis) to each individual by asking and considering

1. Are your Career Goals being met;

2. Are your Developmental Goals being met; and

3. Are your Timing Goals/Expectations being met?

A major clue you have a breakdown somewhere in the TALENTification process, is when talent leaves you and it is a surprise to the supervising manager and the hiring manager (if this is a different person). It is also reflective of a breakdown in the Performance

Review process, as an individual was not being challenged, engaged and/or developed within their respective areas and considered for advancement.

A key aspect of TALENTification is the responsibility of every supervising manager and hiring manager to be cognizant of what each person on their team does, what their growth goals are, and what roles you see that person growing into within the organization. These must also be communicated to the employee. Talent gaps, lacks and losses should be at a minimum if the ACHIEVEMENT process is at work. Learning of an impending employee departure to pursue employment growth opportunities with another employer -- because an employee did not see themselves within your organization or because you failed to articulate your strategic plans, which included them -- is a failure of the TALENTification succession process.

Individuals, likewise, should be aware of the TALENTification process, as well, and feel comfortable communicating with their supervising manager, hiring manager and/or senior leaders regarding their goals/aspirations and whether they feel those are being met.

Business/C-Suite leaders at their respective levels must architect out their immediate, intermediate and long-term talent needs, growth migration patterns of personnel and the ongoing professional development needs for their business enterprise to survive and thrive – including both the technician skills/aptitudes requirements and the professional KSAs to perform the TDR expected.

The degree of culture disruption, productivity disruption and profitability hits an organization takes due to these failures is massive on an annual and global basis. Architect out individual player aspirations for positional efficiency, productivity, profitability and development as it relates to the individual ... align this with succession needs.

3-Deep Mindset

Now, take everything we have presented within the ACHIEVE-MENT process, the TALENTification life cycle and your initiatives on succession and ask what are you really doing to develop the future human-capital bench-strength three levels down from the top (of any position or key player)? Only when you are strategically thinking and executing at a three-deep level are you building a best-in-class organization and building for market dominance for today (first level), tomorrow (second level) and the future (third level)!

And, then reflect back as you evaluate your DEI Model or Processes and ask yourself are we hitting these four core KPI/elements? Four core elements to be considered and executed in the implementation of your DEI-of-TALENTification process:

- One – Implementing and Communicating the Organizations DEI Talent Strategy – **Determine your DEI Strategy**

- Second – Establish the governance structure – Choice of WHAT this will be for you and HOW it is to be executed

- Third – Identify the key metrics to be used and measured for progress/goals – **Clarify that everyone understands**

- Fourth – Empower diversity leaders, champions and advocates to engage everyone – Commitment of whether your people willing & Congruence to your Culture and Values

As you undertake this important Ninth phase of the ACHIEVE-MENT life cycle, always stay focused on how this applies to the TALENT throughout other applications. For an organization, it demands the understanding of each application and how they actually must align as one for ultimate ROI. Identify at each of the following five TALENT considerations what you expect the new talent to do, i.e., TDR. This must be done first because it leads into the next crucial step: what KSAs are required to perform the role (TDR) you plan to put them in:

1. TALENT management of the INDIVIDUAL;

2. TALENT management of career PATHWAYS;

3. TALENT management of critical essential POSITION pathways;

4. TALENT management of secondary support POSITION pathways; and

5. TALENT management of the ORGANIZATION.

Understanding the life cycle of TALENTification is critical and we hope this book helps synthesize what we know about human capital while providing a simplified approach for individuals and organizations to move beyond the carousel of the past.

Chapter Ten

Next Steps And Postmortem

Analysis Of DEI(A)

Next Steps … Post Mortem Analysis – On a regular cycle (Quarterly or Annually) pull together a cross population of DEI key stakeholders (key employees, ERG/EEG leaders, HR team, core business unit leaders and the C-Suite) to discuss where your goals were at the beginning of the year and where are we now? Evaluate how people are participating (voluntarily stepping up and in, is it cross team involvement and participation, are we setting and achieving goals, who is included in the goals and making strides, who is just along for the rind, and who are the outliers) …?

How are we including and celebrating successes along the way? How are we encouraging socialization.

Just pull raw numbers as a gatekeeper to diversity inclusion:

One - What does the diversity of our Present-State organization relevel our make-up to be?

Two - What does the diversity of our Present-State community we can pull employee talent from relevel the make-up to be?

Third - What does the diversity of our Present-State customer base relevel the make-up to be?

These three macro numbers will reveal how diverse reflective you are to the environment around you.

Fourth - Then ask yourself, what does your diversity look like across the organization and from the bottom of the organization to the top?

Review the DEI Strategy and evaluate any adjustments necessary, consider the four core elements to be considered and executed in the DEI-of-TALENTification process discussed at the beginning of the ACHIEVEMENT model and how well are you executing on:

One – Implementing and Communicating the Organizations DEI Talent Strategy

Second – Establish the governance structure

Third – Identify the key metrics to be used and measured for progress/goals

Fourth – Empower diversity leaders, champions and advocates to engage everyone

Remember, "Top-down support is crucial, and bottom-up involvement is critical" to any inclusive DEI talent program, it must be holistic to work, as Professor Lionel **Paolella of the University Of Cambridge, Judge Business School Executive Education** has found through his research, so what does your data reveal about how you are executing.

All next steps aligned with previous KPIs: *Exit Interviews, Benchmarking, and SWOT Analysis against every human-capital need on an individual and organizational level; How does this integrate into Business Plans, Mission Statements and Values; Ensuring Inclusion and Diversity equal to marketplace; Onboarding the Retired Superstars; Etc.*

How will you objectively know what TALENTification DEI great looks like?

The execution, ownership and championing of the ACHIEVE-MENT™ Process; Imagine it were your Mom or Dad, your Brother or Sister, your Daughter or Son, your Niece or Nephew, your Cousin or In-Law … Would you want any of them if willing to participate and could bring value to you and your organization to have an equal opportunity to participate?

The hard reality for many individuals of diversity, is because many of us are hard wired with adult biases or have just evolved to be inclusive of people like us and not recognize that we are *"Judging That Book By the Cover"* without ever seeing what is on the inside, we may in fact be holding others back from greatness and limiting ourselves from a beautiful growth experience.

Goldman Sachs address removing these walls and increasing inclusion of diversity globally through many initiatives, on being Building Allyships among groups and within groups. Their DEI initiatives among many KPIs that work for them, they work to:

- Create opportunities to listen to individuals and groups horizontally and vertically

- Take time to learn about one another and recognize how to leverage one another

- Learn about micro aggressions

- Build empathy & mentoring

- Sponsorship of a great colleague, that can lead to greater diversity and the number of promotions

- Commitment from the top of the Firm downward

- Data analytics will be critical on how you attract, retain and in dealing with attrition

To remain relevant as an organization and as an individual, the analysis of the talent question at the end of any lifecycle is crucial. Whether it's at the end of an individual's work with a team, a work project, etc., or an individual's employment with the organization, an exit interview is critical.

Being able to objectively and without emotion engage in a postmortem exercise to see what lesson-learned experiences can be gleaned is necessary by all involved in the talent process, if in fact, the desired goal is a more efficient ACHIEVEMENT reality.

There are a host of ways to accomplish this. From running the traditional graduate-management course SWOT exercise to a peer review focus group. Whatever the forum, system or tool used for this indexing exercise, it is not about laying blame on human-capital or talent derailments or patting oneself on the back for victories. It is for the uncovering of raw data from which you can make future focused decisions and commitments.

Your culture must value diversity or this entire book and your every endeavor is mere an exercise in futility. Here is a sequence of considerations for an effective checkup:

1. As senior leaders, business owners and talent-management personnel, this postmortem phase is a benchmarking opportunity against your annual Business Plan and Quarterly Business Plan KPIs. Measure how your human-capital bench strength is overall in relationship to what your documents indicate are your priorities, goals and expectations for organizational performance. Now measure in reverse from your documents where your human capital is, from senior-most levels down through critical individual players and critical positions. Forecast out personnel movements due in part to promotions, transfers, attrition, and retirement. Sequence in onboarding timelines for new hires into both critical and support roles, and you will be able to gain a clearer picture of what is working and what, if anything, needs attention and adjustment.

2. If you have a Board of Directors (BOD), consider any implications of the ACHIEVEMENT talent process -- wins and losses -- and the overall analytics that must be presented to your BOD for feedback, validation and approval for any forward growth plans.

3. If you have any outsourced talent partners, assessment partners, training partners, etc. involved in the ACHIEVEMENT talent process, the overall analytics here should also be evaluated for feedback, validation and considerations moving forward.

4. Look at long-term capital improvement or business-development models that the executive team is considering and evaluate how the talent plans are calibrated to sustain and achieve these expectations.

5. Review this past year's ACHIEVEMENT process and benchmark that against your organization's Values, Vision and Mission Statements to ensure alignment.

6. Ensure core stakeholder alignment: review your ACHIEVEMENT model with the senior-most core individual(s) to your organization for input and, more importantly, their feedback on their tenure succession plans, as this unknown variable can be a major game changer and disruptor, if unknown.

7. Market forces should also always be discussed. From vendor supply chains and changes, to major and unknown market competitors in your space, to economic, political and other forces that can be a minor or major influence on your TALENTification process.

Core Stake-Holders
The success and failure of the eleven inter-linked elements in this book, can only come to life if the senior most leader (CEO) buys-into the philosophy, adds their own uniqueness to the formula and then parks this with a senior leader, with direct connection to them as the advocate!
This is a non negotiable…

One of my clients had a major global talent-search firm on retainer. With their background vetting and recommendation, a senior-level individual for a senior-level position was hired. In short order it became evident that the individual could not function or do some of the most elementary of TDRs and was let go. In conversation with the talent-search firm, the firm indicated it was not their responsibility to vet the prospect and the failure to perform was not their responsibility. Needless to say, the retainer relationship ceased to continue.

Another of my clients is in a market that is already competitive for entry-level labor talent. While there can be some degree of automation that can address some of the labor needs, the reality is that a human being must be in the talent equation. The new ACHIEVE-MENT challenges will come when three new globally branded businesses announced that they will be locating and building major distribution centers in their market. Knowing that information in advance of them coming, gives you ample time to solidify your ACHIEVEMENT process and creates an environment that makes it hard for others to attract your "Superstars", your "Developing Stars" and your "Future Stars."

As a Post Mortem, it is good business to always pause and evaluate all talent outcomes, good or bad, for lessons learned and accelerated success continually.

Remember, the overall employee experience is shaped and determined by how you (individually and organizationally) manage your side of each of the ACHIEVEMENT lifecycle phases and what the individual employee receives, sees, observes, and internalizes as their EXPERIENCE along the way. Every touchpoint from the organization, whether intentional or unintentional, whether overt or not, still shapes the experience an individual has within the work environment.

Whether you are in a leadership capacity, business ownership or employee, there should be a fiercely objective set of analytics or a human resources dashboard that reveals where any individual lies in regard to talent capacity (as both a technician in their job role and functionality, as well as overall professional acumen and development) that clearly indicates the next talent growth initiative expectations for measurement. Ultimate talent development, integration and growth should be about elevating every individual to be as agile, nimble, flexible, and proactive as characteristics of the Talent Development pipeline in producing internal human capital 24/7.

Inclusion driven by culture and diversity acquired by talent development for healthy balanced organization …

With an embraced ACHIEVEMENT model by all key stakeholders within your organization, it now begs the question of how the organization is attracting the best talent available and leveraging that talent for the wellness of the organization. From the beginning, make sure you continuously evaluate how your culture drives inclusion and diversity. Continuous observation at each level of the ACHIEVEMENT process must be undertaken as a postmortem. Evaluate how your talent demographics reflect the population indices of your marketplace.

As an example, in any geography on the planet there are sample data sets available from academic research bodies and governmental agencies.

I work with a national organization in the United States of America and, in any state, there are data sets that break down that state's population index, from age zero through 100, and by gender, social economics, education, ethnicity and zip code. Evaluate that data for a diversity index span, and then benchmark this against the population demographics of your organization – this will provide you a simple means to gauging whether your organization is reflective and inclusive based upon the diversity of your market, your industry, and your geography. To be relevant in tomorrow's global economy, ask yourself whether your TALENTification process is reflective of the marketplace you serve now and tomorrow?

You can retool the need for a more aggressive and accountable inclusive organization into each of the individual phases of the ACHIEVEMENT process. Inclusion is about creating and embracing pathways for acquiring, onboarding, developing and retaining the best talent, regardless of how one's name is spelled. **Make no mistake though:**

1. TALENTification is not about making an inclusive space for people on your team who are not worthy and are not willing to dedicate and apply themselves equal to the best talent within the organization. Inclusion and diversity is not undertaken to merely be able to have a rainbow picture and checkmarks on a ledger to appease the body politic.

2. TALENTification is not about making an inclusive space for people on your team that merely lean on their diversity to get a

seat in the organization as they say and are incapable of delivering the ROI for the organization. Inclusion and diversity are not undertaken to merely be able to have a rainbow picture and checkmarks on a ledger to appease the body politic.

3. TALENTification is about creating an inclusive space for people who want to embrace your Values, Vision and Mission Statement, not change them for their own personal agenda. Inclusion and diversity is not undertaken to merely be able to have a rainbow picture and checkmarks on a ledger to appease the body politic.

Creating an inclusive environment will actually create greater value to the individuals within the organization and greater shareholder value. Incorporate strategies, processes and procedures that embrace inclusion throughout your organization and instill a stronger lifeblood.

As the ACHIEVEMENT process is reviewed and analyzed for effectiveness and points of recalibration for greater ROI, it is important that each level of human capital check back in on the process and participate regularly in an audit activity to ensure that the **TALENTification roles of its human capital or talent pool are being proactively executed:**

1. Senior Leaders (EDP Level) own the Vision and Macro architect roles;

2. HR Hiring Managers & Talent Mgt. Personnel (LDP Level) own the roles of Ambassadors, Educators & Accountability Compliance Partners;

3. Supervising Managers (MDP Level) serve as the frontline Implementation Executors, Developers, and Coaches;

4. Personnel/Employees at Large have the responsibility of being Advocates, Participants and Influencers at all levels in embracing the ACHIEVEMENT Model process;

5. Outsourced Partners must assume the associated roles that they are engaged to fulfill within the ACHIEVEMENT process, whether that is serving in the role of execution, compliance or accountability partners; and

6. Vendor/Service Partners should also be acquainted with the organization's TALENTification ACHIEVEMENT process to assist with their best-practice abilities, where applicable.

And as you evaluate in the *Postmortem Next Steps Analysis*, consider ... TALENTification also extends to the SUPERSTARs (See Chapter Eight - *Remember how we established the level of human-capital personnel as STARS: Superstars, Rising Stars, Developing Stars, Crashing Stars and Unknown Stars*), who have been organically raised, developed and celebrated within an organization and then retire.

These SUPERSTARS retire from an organization with immense KSAs having demonstrated excellence in execution of TDRs, losing the organization untold costs. The knowledge drain of these lost human-capital assets, in respect to their institutional and industry knowledge and wisdom, can be a massive loss to an organization's culture and identity. Best-in-Class organizations that accelerate the ACHIEVEMENT model must consider and explore ways to harness that WISDOM within these individuals as MENTORS or ADVISORS to the next generation of Superstars, Rising Stars and Developing Stars.

This can be a massive force multiplier to human- capital initiatives, from recruiting to retention and from onboarding to sequenced talent development. Imagine inviting ONLY retired SUPERSTARS for

1. Outside-In Mentoring – Partner up retired Superstars with next generation Superstars, Evolving Stars and Developing Stars via a managed HR/Talent Development Team dynamic, in a non-supervising role to individuals and be at-call Mentors or Advisors to employees.

2. Outside In Mentoring – Partner retired Superstars, whom the organization has vetted, with those who want more developmental coaching; have a contact list of go-to people.

3. Outside-In Mentoring – Partner up retired Superstars with others to be an additional reinforcement to the career pathway developmental needs for growth

4. Inside-Out Mentoring – As situations dictate, reach out to proven Superstars who understand your culture and people dynamics when organizational effectiveness can be enhanced.

5. Inside-Out Mentoring – Consider, as additional consultation touchpoints to key executives and even Board Members, leveraging the WISDOM of the ages for faster, greater, more efficient future decisions and actions.

6. Inside-Out Mentoring – As an unexpected opening occurs within your organization and a key position is vacated, the urgency and stress can be mitigated by accessing a proven veteran to stop back in temporarily, so you can engage in focused talent acquisition for the opening. By doing this, you can avoid that rushed, stressed, pressured need to fill an opening with just anyone that feels or looks good on the surface; which may be an intermediate and or long-term mistake.

Leveraging (in a very controlled manner) the talent of Superstars who retire, and creating a pathway whereby they can be invited back in an "at need" basis, can become a human-capital talent accelerator to greater market success.

Create a macro guide or check list of inclusive best-practices that everyone at every level with the organizations can benchmark their own behaviors, actions, comments and commitments against to ensure the culture and organization you have, seek or desire to maintain is always strengthened by every action and initiative and that no one consciously (bias) or unconsciously (bias) allows for great talent to be pushed aside and be made to feel unwelcomed. You can get insights from several global trade associations such as:

- www.shrm.org - SHRM - The Voice of All Things Work
- www.td.org – ATD | The World's Largest Talent Development Association | ATD

As you undertake this important Tenth phase of the ACHIEVE-MENT lifecycle, always stay focused on how this applies to the TAL-ENT throughout other applications. For an organization, it demands the understanding of each application and how they actually must align as one for ultimate ROI. Identify at each of the following five TALENT considerations what you expect the new talent to do, i.e., TDR. This must be done first because it leads into the next crucial step: what KSAs are required to perform the role (TDR) you plan to put them in:

1. TALENT management of the INDIVIDUAL;

2. TALENT management of career PATHWAYS;

3. TALENT management of critical essential POSITION pathways;

4. TALENT management of secondary support POSITION pathways; and

5. TALENT management of the ORGANIZATION.

Understanding the life cycle of TALENTification is critical and we hope this book helps synthesize what we know about human capital while providing a simplified approach for individuals and organizations to move beyond the carousel of the past.

Chapter Eleven

Teach The Organization DEI(A)-Of-TALENTification

TEACH TALENTification Relaunch/Evolution – DEI-of-TAL-ENTification is not a onetime program or event, it is a continuous journey, it is every experience we have within and outside of an organizational structure. All next steps aligned with previous KPIs: *Best Practice Management, Lessons Learned Implementations; Benchmark against industry or trade association analytics; recalibration as appropriate; The C-Suite consideration; Etc.*

DEI(A) is about the inclusion of all and the exclusion of none.

DEI(A) should not be code for gender inequality or ethnicity inequality or etc., it should be about the reality that diversity as I have stated in my writings and keynote work, truly is your strategic advantage and is therefore your strategic imperative!

For the past 20 years I have been building emerging leadership programs for the growth demographics of today and tomorrow; Emerging Women In Leadership, Emerging Minorities in Leadership, Emerging Young Professionals for many leading trade associations and businesses.

An example. Ultimately everyone owns DEI just as everyone owns Safety within an organization, it must be that simple as a mental baseline within the organization. Here is where the Advocates and Champions at every level that you have embedded strategically will yield celebration and success in a stronger organization – from ERGs to frontline employees/colleagues/associates to the executive team and BOD. This is not an initiative or something to be done, because it makes us look good or makes us feel virtuous, it is smart sound business.

This is really about celebrating your greatness as an organization. Celebrating the "wins" you have along the way each day, week, month and year. It is about creating an environment or culture that sustains these steps, as if they have been institutionalized and no one can delete, take away or diminish any of the eleven phases. You can always add and enhance these phases, but you can never take away. And it is about the ability to own up to all of the gaps, cracks, shortcomings and weaknesses, both on an individual and organizational level, and address them head on for greater effectiveness and efficiencies. No longer allowing the egos to protect the deficits that corrupt the TALENT process.

When individuals of diverse backgrounds (which we all have), in their own way and on their own level, own these eleven phases as it pertains to an individual organizations Value System, then you know your organization is buying into and living the TAL-ENTififcation Model.

This holds true for society and civilizations, for our history students. It is when diverse people are aligned with common purpose and language that great things can be and will be accomplished.

TALENTification is about creating the analytics by which success is determined, measured and maintained. The adage, what gets measured, gets attention, is not just a saying.

So, what is the reality of your organization undertaking this TAL-ENTification process, and more importantly, of maintaining this model as you re-launch annually for an evolving, growing, engaging reality?

Remember the Gallup organization study we shared in the beginning of this ACHIEVEMENT™ Process discussion, of thousands of businesses, from small entrepreneurial businesses to major global enterprises (including Federal, State and Metro government agencies) to assess the level of engagement of personnel. What they found is consistent with what I have experienced globally for the past three decades:

1. **56** percent of surveyed respondents indicated that they were **"disengaged/complacent"** in the workplace. These respondents are neither positive nor negative, good nor bad, proactive nor reactive; they are influenced by others and the behaviors they

exhibit are the TALENTification norms of their leaders, peers and organization.

2. **15** percent of surveyed respondents indicated that they were "**actively disengaged**" in the workplace. These respondents have learned how to play the game; play the system; outlive probationary periods before the real them shows up to work; manipulate others; play passive-aggressively; identified the least that they can do, so no one can ever terminate them, etc. Sadly, this is due to an inept talent process that has not grown true leaders to engage, hold accountable or stand up to these cancerous parasites in an organization.

3. **29** percent of surveyed respondents indicated that they were "**actively engaged**" in the workplace. These respondents are the producers in your organization and the talent players of today and tomorrow. Build upon them, invest in them, celebrate them and you will motivate more of the 56 percenters to be like them. And when you re-launch, always have them vested into the process and the evolution of a culture of TALENTification will become automatic.

Remember, the overall employee experience is shaped and determined by how you (individually and organizationally) manage your side of each of the ACHIEVEMENT lifecycle phases and what the individual employee receives, sees, observes, and internalizes as their EXPERIENCE along the way. Every touchpoint from the organization, whether intentional or unintentional, whether overt or not, still shapes the experience an individual has within the work environment.

So, make this an annual experience, on an individual level, to internally audit for talent evaluation. Do this across business units and organizationally to assess talent and celebrate the continuous life-cycle process of TALENTification.

As you re-launch, you can have strategically placed champions/advocates in every business unit and across all geographical locations to ensure old habits do not persist and that new forward-focused TALENTification processes are the norm of the day. These champions/advocates can assist on a local level to ensure consistencies and implementation, and can serve as immediate feedback loops to key leadership. These champions/advocates can work in concert with the human-resource professionals and learning-and-development teams within your organization (for larger enterprises) to ensure the ACHIEVEMENT process is embodied in everything the organization does.

Alignment of all capital assets drives organizational effectiveness and success. Alignment of all human capital, at every level, is the critical asset that everything is derived from.

The pivot point for human-capital success is the art and science of crafting an indelible culture and organization that allows you to FIND Talent, GET Talent, KEEP Talent, GROW Talent and RE-GENERATE the ACHIEVEMENT lifecycle that is TALENTification!

A key aspect of TALENTification is the responsibility of every supervising manager and hiring manager to be cognizant of what each person on their team does, what their growth goals are, and what roles you see that person growing into within the organization. These must also be communicated to the employee. Talent gaps, lacks and losses should be at a minimum if the ACHIEVEMENT process is at work. Learning of an impending employee departure to pursue employment growth opportunities with another employer -- because an employee did not see themselves within your organization or because you failed to articulate your strategic plans, which included them -- is a failure of the TALENTification succession process.

Individuals, likewise, should be aware of the TALENTification process, as well, and feel comfortable communicating with their supervising manager, hiring manager and/or senior leaders regarding their goals/aspirations and whether they feel those are being met.

Business/C-Suite leaders at their respective levels must architect out their immediate, intermediate and long-term talent needs, growth migration patterns of personnel and the ongoing professional development needs for their business enterprise to survive and thrive – including both the technician skills/aptitudes requirements and the professional KSAs to perform the TDR expected.

The degree of culture disruption, productivity disruption and profitability hits an organization takes due to these failures is massive on an annual and global basis. Architect out individual player aspirations for positional efficiency, productivity, profitability and development as it relates to the individual ... align this with succession needs.

With the gained insights of the first ten phases of the ACHIEVE-MENT process, and before you reboot and continue with the eleventh phase, another consideration in elevating the impact and ROI is to evaluate how the senior-most leaders of your organization embrace and engage TALENTification. I call this the **C-Suite Consideration.**

The established hierarchy of a business model or an organizational chart that has been taught and is generally accepted is that there are core business spheres of responsibility in any organization. The larger the organization or business enterprise is, the more established this architecture becomes. Your organization, whether local or global, may vary in what spheres of influence and responsibility or roles and titles you may have as your senior bench or C-Suite. It does not matter what working names or titles you may give to such spheres (roles, positions, titles, etc.), they are always the same –Traditionally, these are the power centers where decisions are made and lives are affected. The uniqueness of your business may also drive C-Suite positions for you that may not be represent for another business. As an example, you may have a Chief Manufacturing Officer or a Chief Distribution Officer ...

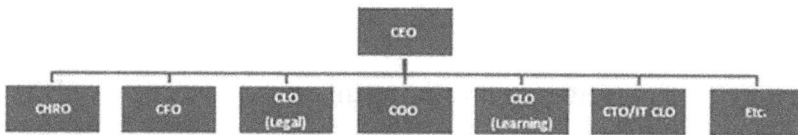

Consider is this senior level architecture reflective of the diverse and rich segmentations of your Present-State and Future-State organization. The research papers abound on how a diverse BOD, ELT, Senior Leadership and entire labor force impacts greater profitability and revenue streams to an organization – what does your balance sheet look like, there is a DEI correlation.

As the leader of a business (business Owner, President or CEO), typically this C-Suite architecture becomes your inner circle for immediate, intermediate and long-term decisions. What the C-Suite Consideration suggests, in the new TALENTification world, is a massive paradigm shift in all future decision-making. Keep the wide band of C-Suite spheres/positions in the organizational chart if you like, and there may be times when the entire diverse group should exist and be in play, but as we now live in a global marketplace, no matter how small or local you actually believe you play, the core leverage you have and the only way to ensure survival and thriving abilities is to have at the core only FOUR C-Suite Considerations.

These four considerations are the future drivers to everything that you as a CEO need to achieve ACHIEVEMENT-

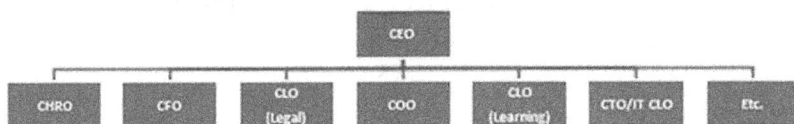

As the CEO, no matter what your organization is, you have only two assets in the global marketplace of tomorrow, *Finance* and *Human Capital*.

These two must be seated at either side of you 24/7. The third C-Suiter is the drilled down essential category of what your business really is. If it's manufacturing, then Chief Manufacturing Officer (CMO); if it's technology, the Chief Technology Officer (CTO; if it's information, then it's Chief Information Office; if it's agri or farming, then it's Chief Farming Officer ..., you get the point.

All other C-Suite spheres or roles are designed to accelerate these highest C-suiters' core ability to serve the TALENTification model, the business (it has its own life as well), and ultimately the CEO (Business Owner, President or whatever working title one has as the titular head of the entity). Keep in mind, everyone has an "agenda" and every C-Suite individual represents a significant piece of your business. Draw upon and consider their counsel to you and others, but ensure that their "agenda" never forsakes or trumps the FOUR C-Suite Considerations.

With a like-minded, fluid group of personalities, your organization can be well served by having a diverse, inclusive and engaged Advisory Board or BOD. These, too, should be involved and engaged accordingly into the ACHIEVEMENT model.

As you undertake this important Eleventh and final phase (before you re-loop and flow through the process as an actual never-ending process) of the ACHIEVEMENT lifecycle, always stay focused on how this applies to the TALENT throughout other applications. For an organization, it demands the understanding of each application and how they actually must align as one for ultimate ROI. Identify at each of the following five TALENT considerations what you expect the new talent to do, i.e., TDR. This must be done first because it leads into the next crucial step: what KSAs are required to perform the role (TDR) you plan to put them in:

1. TALENT management of the INDIVIDUAL;

2. TALENT management of career PATHWAYS;

3. TALENT management of critical essential POSITION pathways;

4. TALENT management of secondary support POSITION pathways; and

5. TALENT management of the ORGANIZATION.

Understanding the life cycle of TALENTification is critical and we hope this book helps synthesize what we know about human capital while providing a simplified approach for individuals and organizations to move beyond the carousel of the past.

Chapter Twelve
Re-Launch/Evolution

<u>The Disruption Interruption Point Curve Is Your</u>
<u>Never Ending What's Next That Impacts & Influences</u>
<u>Dei(A) And Every Kpi Can Impact & Influence Dei(A)</u>

TALENTification – The 11 Elements to Execution and ACHIEVE-
MENT of the Talent Management Model for a Healthy, Sustained
& Engaged Organization and how the Disruption/Interruption
Business Cycle™ & The Disruption/Interruption Points™ (DIPs) im-
pact Your Ultimate Success!

The *Disruption/Interruption Business Cycle™* & *The Disruption/Inter-*
ruption Points™ (DIPs) that influence every aspect your life, business
and the ACHIEVEMENT™ Process

Every decade for the past fifty years has had a massive global reboot occurrence. These shifts have created Change on every level of people's personal and professional lives. With it, many organizations have imploded, merged to survive, and struggled through the tough reboot; few have leveraged as **Changeformationalists** what others saw as Change and were able to accelerate to greatness and transform – DEI is one of those DIPs of opportunity.

In my groundbreaking business and success book, *CHANGEFOR-MATIONAL: Change Happens & Transformations OCCUR, WIN BY BEING CHANGEFORMATIONAL!* I discuss the DIPs model and your ability to understand all three elements of that bell-curve will create DEI of ACHIEVEMENT successes that will make you the benchmark of excellence others strive to emulate!

Think about the last few Global Reboots and how it has shaped the complexion of the labor force globally and where you are:

1. 1990s – Dot-com companies experience uncontrolled growth and then the bubble implodes.

2. 2001 – 911 World Trade Center attack, impending Middle East Wars, and Civil Uprising "Springs"

3. 2008/10 – World Recession; Lehman Brothers and like businesses file for bankruptcy and the USA real estate market implodes.

4. 2020 – Chinese Corona Virus, Global Pandemic Reboot & the Bitcoin market scandals/implosion

5. ? – What's the next big Change/DIP event?

Your ability to forecast and plan strategically ahead of any DIUP and or to leverage your diverse human capital in the facer of a DIP, allows you to survive the immediate and come out the others side and thrive. That ability to see change and leverage it to be transformational is what is meant by being CHANGEFORMATIONAL™!

Bringing the concept of Change stimulants or KPIs closer to where you live and work, consider what the Change inflection points are in life, business, and society and how people respond (logic-based), or react (emotion-based), to each.

For some the entire discussion of DEI has been a DIP with genuine and disingenuous implications.

Allow me to illustrate a way to look at the Changes in our lives and the Transformations you may need to undertake. In business, I call this the **Disruption/Interruption Business Cycle™**.

Below is a model I have adapted and transformed into a life model as well as business model.

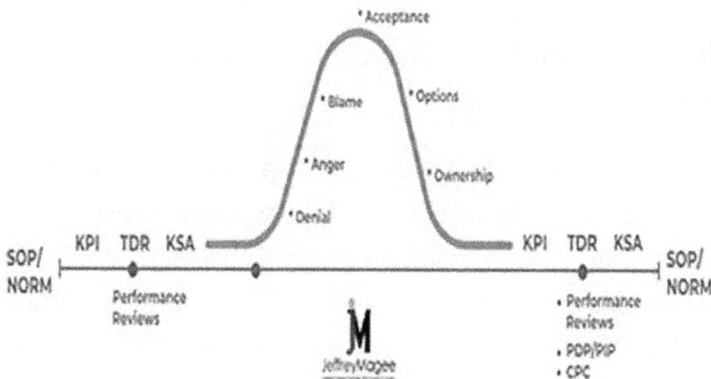

First, recognize that most people (at least the 80-percenters from Chapter Five), just want to live and operate within the flat lines of either the left or right side. The flat line represents norms, routines and expectations; these are the KPIs that you live within. Once you know what is expected from you, (KPIs), then you associate the corresponding Tasks, Duties and Responsibilities (TDR) of an activity or a job, etc. to those KPIs. Next, draw upon or seek the Knowledge, Skills and Abilities (KSA) you must possess to survive and operate. In a job, you receive performance feedback or reviews along this flat line, as indicated by the first dot on the above bell-curve flat line.

The **Disruption/Interruption Business Cycle** then illustrates at the second dot on the flat line where a disruption or interruption may occur that causes a Change inflection point in your life. To understand when Change may appear or to even anticipate it, empowers you to be able to consider ways to expedite your time in the initial Change interruption left side of the curve that derails most people and organizations. The ability to reach the top of the bell-curve as efficiently, respectfully and quickly as possible, allows you to apply Transformational thinking to accelerate across the top of the curve and down the right side to **Changeformational** outcomes and new realities.

The derailer for most individuals and organizations is at that point (the dot) on the flat line where the interruption or disruption happens and the bell curve becomes an uphill challenge. When Change presents itself during your time on the flat line, you have been conditioned to waste time and invest a percentage of time at each point from the bottom of the curve to the top left.

The dot at the beginning of any upward curve is the **Disruption Interruption Point/DIP™**, and it can be constructive and positive or unforeseen, critical and negative.

When you can "anticipate" impending **DIPs** and position yourself and others to be prepared for them, you can leverage that dip for wins, and become **Changeformational**.

For most people and organizations, when they first encounter Change or especially shocking encounters, they immediately go into DENIAL. This then derails logical thinking and requires Change intervention and engagement endeavors – what a waste of time in the end.

Then, when this stage does not create the desired outcome, the next phase is spent attempting to avoid the new reality by exploding in ANGER – what a waste of time in the end.

Then, when ANGER does not create the desired outcome, the next phase is spent attempting to avoid the new reality by wanting to throw someone under the bus, as a deflection exercise in BLAME – what a waste of time in the end.

Transformation is about getting to ACCEPTANCE, as fast and prudently as possible, so energies can be aligned and focused upon OPTIONS and OWNERSHIP for **Changeformational** implementation and execution.

With ACCEPTANCE, comes a universal energy, a belief that we are all in this together. In essence, everyone has some degree, albeit differing degrees, of skin in the game. This collective buy-in takes place so you can let go of the left side of the bell curve and awaken to the vast opportunities of the right side of the bell curve.

The **Changeformational** leader or observer can recognize (anticipate, intuitively read, recognize, observe, assess), from within the flat line of the left side of the **Disruption/Interruption Business Cycle** what's on the horizon and, by Transformational action, institute systems, processes and procedures to minimize the impending Change stimulant, even avoid it in its entirety, while others are consumed by it!

The Transformational activities are aligned on the right side of the bell curve and float line to bring everyone forward with a sense of confidence in what the future holds and what is expected from them.

Now, let's accelerate everything you just read. To take **Changeformational** to the next level, look at each of the past **DIPs** (whether negative or positive), as what you must have on your Dashboard. And even better is when you can forecast what the **DIPs** are. For example ...

As the Trajectory Code V-Diagram above projects, there are what I call five levels of behavior that everyone will experience leaving Point A; there is no stopping the progression. The goal is to have insight and knowledge to always ensure that you are applying those behaviors in an AC Trajectory and, when you do so, you will always be in **Changeformational** Transformation mode. If you are not paying attention and consciously aware, those same five behaviors can actually propel you in an AB Trajectory, and Change will happen to you. You will be playing in others' games of life.

The five levels of Behavior.

As you leave Point A, we are all trained/educated in how to do what we do, I call this a Behavior (the conscious state or Level One). From here, as you see in the diagram that evolves into a Habit (the unconscious state or Level 2). Over time we become so comfortable in what we do, how we do it, and why we do it the way we do that it now becomes a Personal SOP (Autopilot state or Level Three). Once you reach this state, with no accountability and feedback stimulus, we take Ownership (Personalized state or Level Four) of our actions. We now build a protective state around us and what we do. Our emotions play defense to any outside suggestions or questioning (Emotional state or Level Five). In the Trajectory Code V-Diagram AC-Trajectory application, this can have devastating consequences. Likewise, these same five levels of Behavior will actualize no matter what. Now if we arm ourselves consciously at each level, we can leverage this as Transformative in nature – every time.

You can embrace this concept and embrace the ACHIEVEMENT™ Process, introduce it to your organization and incorporate it into your cultural DNA in many ways. One, is to consider what I have learned from every successful business owner, organizational leader, military General and Command-Sergeants-Major, association executive, solo-entrepreneur and truly powerful subject-matter experts whom I've had the honor to work with for three-plus decades.

I have created this checklist of the **SEVEN PERFORMANCE TRAITS** or **ORGANIZATIONAL DNA** to high-impact performance execution. As you benchmark against each, the *"application"* of each is exactly that: how do you live it, demonstrate it, exhibit it.

1. *You and your organization through the DEI of ACHIEVEMENT process* - Develops, maintains, and fosters a healthy atmosphere for a forward-oriented constructive positive __ATTITUDE__ or, a climate of positive self, internally and externally, among others!

   Are you having fun? Is your environment conducive to engagement, development, and healthy challenges? Do you and your colleagues have a hunger for growth, continuous improvement and celebration, or is the psychology (attitude) one of complacency, routine and defensiveness.

2. *You and your organization through the DEI of ACHIEVEMENT process* - Understands how __PASSION__ feeds __OWNERSHIP__ and continuously place yourself and others into the circle for victory and never-ending enthusiasm for self and what one projects towards others as their body of work – this is the baseline for performance execution.

   Research shows a direct line between people who are passionate about the things they do and the people that they are able to engage and increased productivity, profitability and loyalty.

   Find out what people are passionate about, and you will have a window into what people are going to commit to and pursue, as opposed to what they won't do or resist. If you want people to be more engaged and freely assume ownership of "X" (tasks, duties, responsibilities), then tie that into their passion.

3. *You and your organization through the DEI of ACHIEVEMENT process* - The unwavering objective ability to assess oneself and

others to ensure that the __PLAYER CAPABILITY INDEX__ level of oneself and others is always ahead of market needs.

It's human nature to make allowances for those we know and like, while looking for shortcomings in those we don't like. It is paramount to the ACHIEVEMENT process and to success to have objective analytics to hold opinions in check and to operate from sound, objective data for never-ending capacity development. The ability to scope tasks, delegation, new project needs, job description drafting and interviewing is essential for success. For personal and professional coaching, mentoring and accelerating others to attain aspirations can be scientifically facilitated through Player Capability Indexing.

4. *You and your organization through the DEI of ACHIEVEMENT process* - All commitments, undertakings, and actions are compliant with the five integrated __MISSION__ STATEMENTS__ of all balanced individuals and organizations. Each interdependent of one another, yet dependent upon one another.

   Think of a Mission Statement as the GPS or roadmap for every endeavor, action, behavior, commitment and collaboration that an individual or groups of people undertake. A clearly defined Mission Statement, even if reduced to a mantra, provides clear guidance to where everyone is going together.

5. You and your organization through the DEI of ACHIEVEMENT process - With these four foundational elements in play, the ability to execute decision-making becomes our accelerator for success. A fundamental differentiator between successful people and organizations and others is that successful people and organizations do what others hesitate to do. This comes

down to performance execution: decision-making. The fluid ability to facilitate a decision flow through the four-step __STOP__ DECISION-MAKING MATRIX® is critical!

If you have a means, formula, process or tool to ensure sound, balanced decision-making and execution, then continue with what works for you. This is an essential element of the TAL-ENTification lifecycle process. If you lack an effective objective approach, then the STOP formula created for our global clients in the 1990s still serves as a turnkey, powerful approach.

6. *You and your organization through the DEI of ACHIEVEMENT process* - Pulling away from the crowd. The ability to accentuate one's __UNIQUE SELLING FEATURE (your WHAT factors)__ and __UNIQUE SERVICE FEATURE (your HOW factors)__ (USFx2) distinguishes you from others. There are four elementary ways to position yourself to project to others a more value proposition than what they presently have or can get elsewhere. Performance execution is dependent upon your ability to finesse these to outperform others.

There are four core ways you do this in human-capital management and business deliverables to ensure that your human capital is always striving for maximum performance and how to be:

a. __BETTER__

b. __FASTER__

c. __DIFFERENT__

d. __COST EFFECTIVE__

Our consumer mind is calibrated to make buying decisions or change our buying behaviors only when something new raises our awareness that there are ways to have an increased quality of life or experience by something that is BETTER, FASTER, DIFFERENT and/or more COST EFFECTIVE than what we presently have. We can apply this same model in how we address human-capital endeavors and the ACHIEVEMENT process. If we are to attract, engage, grow and retain great talent, then always look for ways that you can help individuals attain their life goals in a BETTER, FASTER, DIFFERENT and/or more COST-EFFECTIVE way than any other market option. Challenge those who wish to associate with you, be around you or be a part of your organization to answer how, by hiring them or interacting with them, will the/ be BETTER, FASTER, DIFFERENT and or more COST EFFECTIVE than anyone else you could select and engage?

7. *You and your organization through the DEI of ACHIEVEMENT process* - Recognizing that how one talks internally frames one's operating belief system for any given moment in time. That internal dialogue directs the outward behavior that others can see, monitor, and benchmark. This self-talk can be likened to an internal BOD. Imagine making a fist with your hand, as if you were holding a list of individuals who influence you. Would that be a powerful fist of performance-execution-oriented people or a group of excuse makers for maintaining the status quo a little longer? I call this your __MASTER__MIND__. The never-ending process of encircling oneself with mental, positive references ensures you will accelerate your performance ability *(for more on this one performance idea go*

to www.ProfessionalPerformanceMagazine.com and download edition V.15, I. 1, and read page 21).

The truly cutting-edge, leading-edge, bleeding-edge (or whatever you wish to call them) individuals and organizations are the best of the best. Top organizations demonstrate these characteristics and much more. As you now complete the initial blueprint of the TALENTification process and continue forward with these eleven phases on a never-ending journey, here are a few ideas on what you can do, right now, to ensure you don't backslide and you always live oriented toward the future for greatness:

1. There are affinity organizations and associations for every DEI entity and individual you can think of, connect with them, align with them and allow them to serve as an accelerated subject-matter-expert to you; invite them to step up, step in and be your strategic ally for their constituents in your DEI initiatives;

2. Share copies of this book with others in your organization (www.JeffreyMagee.com);

3. Create a best-practice group to champion these ideas within your organization;

4. Identify one person in your talent pipeline to own this concept and initiate as a TALENTification Ambassador;

5. Explore bringing the Author into your organization/association for a powerful **KEYNOTE;**

6. Explore bringing the Author into your organization/association for a powerful **TALENT-DEVELOPMENT program(s)** at the Executive, Leadership and Management levels;

7. Explore bringing the Author into your organization/association for a **COACHING** program(s) at the Executive, Leadership and Management levels;

8. Benchmark your current talent-development and succession-management initiatives and professional endeavors against *The 11 Elements to Execution and ACHIEVEMENT of the Talent-Management Model for a Healthy, Sustained & Engaged Organization;*

9. Celebrate specific wins globally within your organization and identify ways to expand these wins on a local level.

TALENTification provides you, the individual and the organizational enterprise, with the ability to go as far and fast as your dreams can take you!

TALENTification – The 11 Elements to Execution and ACHIEVE-MENT of the Talent Management Model for a Healthy, Sustained & Engaged Organization!

You can embrace this concept, by identifying how it is being embraced and advocated by:

1. How am **I** advocating the *DEI of* ACHIEVEMENT process in my personal activities?

2. How are **key influencers** within the organization advocating the *DEI of* ACHIEVEMENT process in their daily activities?

3. How are the **HR stakeholders** within the organization advocating the *DEI of* ACHIEVEMENT process in their daily activities?

4. How are the **Senior stakeholders** within the organization advocating the *DEI of* ACHIEVEMENT process in their daily activities?

5. How are the **Terrorists** within the organization advocating or passive-aggressively undermining the *DEI of* ACHIEVEMENT process in their daily activities?

6. How are the **Most-Tenured stakeholders** within the organization, who, feel insulated from demotion or termination

advocating or passive-aggressively working to undermine the *DEI of* ACHIEVEMENT process in their daily activities?

7. How are the **Next Generation of Leaders** within the organization advocating the *DEI of* ACHIEVEMENT process in their daily activities?

8. How are the **Next Generation BEYOND the Next Generation of Leaders** (go three levels deep) within the organization advocating the *DEI of* ACHIEVEMENT process in their daily activities?

9. How are the members of your **Employee Resource Group** or **Employee Engagement Groups** or **Diversity Networking Group** within the organization advocating the *DEI of* ACHIEVEMENT process in their daily activities?

These are critical levels of your organization to observe to get a read on your talent pipeline, the DEI-of-ACHIEVEMENT™ process and the level of TALENTification taking place.

Final Thought

Be very cautious of any one individual being placed or assuming a lead role with DEI(A) and misusing it for personal agendas or re-writing their views of history. As well be very cognizant of any one individual being elevated into a role or position of authority, when their resume yells no credentials. As this will be a massive toxic implosion to your VALUES, organization and will most definitely be the root of a cancer that WILL bring your organization down!

About The Author

Dr. Jeffrey Magee
CBE, CSP, CMC, PDM

... has been called one of today's leading "**Leadership & Marketing Strategists.**" Jeff is the Author of more than 20 books, three college graduate management text books, four best sellers, and is the Publisher of PERFORMANCE/P360 Magazine (www. ProfessionalPerformanceMagazine.com), former Co-Host of the national business entrepreneur program on Catalyst Business Radio (http://www.catalystbusinessradio.com/index.php), and a Human Capital Developer for more than twenty years with www. JeffreyMagee.com.

Professional Credentials:

Magee is committed to professional excellence for you his client and his on-going certification credentials are significant. Along with advanced degrees, he is a Certified Board Executive **(CBE)**, Certified Speaking Professional **(CSP)**, a Certified Management Consultant **(CMC)**, and a Certified Professional Direct Marketer **(PDM)**.

Experience:

Dr. Jeffrey Magee brings over two decades of Executive and Corporate Development expertise, with the last decade working in both the start-up to mature-growth market business sector and with differing State National Guard Adjutant Generals across America. Jeff has and does maintain long term clients working with Association and Organizations at the Board level and across the C-Suite. Beyond this, the importance of working with an organizations entire Human Capital platform from on-boarding, integration, and sustained engagement is critical for an organization's health blue-print. Jeff works with organizations (profit and not-for-profit, private and public sector) in the multi-million-dollar earnings market through to six-billion-dollar earnings market.

Understanding the reality of hard work ethics and drive from an early age, raised on a farm, Jeff started his first business at age 15 and sold it before going to college. By age 24, he was recognized by American Home Products a Fortune 500 company as its top salesman in the nation, while at the same time becoming the youngest certified sales instructor for the **Dale Carnegie Sales Course**. After experiencing downsizing in 1907, he went on to work as a sales associate for the nation's largest educational and youth advertising/marketing firm, Target Marketing, and was promoted to Vice President of Sales and Chief Operating Officer within two years.

MODULE ONE - Reinventing the Fundamentals of Managerial-Leadership Effectiveness: Performance Execution™
By - Dr. Jeffrey Magee, CBE/CSP/CMC/PDM @ DrJeffSpeaks@aol.com
www.JeffreyMagee.com and www.ProfessionalPerformanceMagazine.com

Recognitions:

He has been recognized as one of the **"Ten Outstanding Young Americans"** (TOYA) by the U.S. Junior Chamber of Commerce, and twice selected to represent the United States at the World Congress as a Leadership Speaker (Cannes, France and Vienna, Austria). A three-term President of the Oklahoma Speakers Association and twice awarded their Professional Speaker Member of the Year, today, the Chapter's outstanding member of the year is awarded the *"Jeff Magee Member of the Year Award."* Jeff served for four years as an appointed Civil Service Commissioner (Judge) for the City/County of Tulsa Oklahoma, before relocating to Montana.

Work History/Today:

Today, Magee is the author of the nationally syndicated "Managerial-Leadership" column targeted towards business owners and the C-Suite that you may have seen in your local business newspaper and serves as the publisher of *Professional Performance Magazine/ PERFORMANCE360* – a Quarterly success achievement publication with editorial contributions for the World's leading personalities.

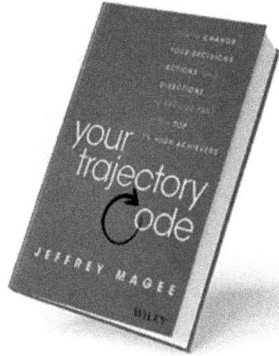

Jeff is the author of more than 20 leadership, performance, and sells books that have been transcribed into multiple languages including four best-sellers. In fact, his text, *Yield Management* has been a #1 selling graduate management school textbook with CRC Press, while *The Sales Training Handbook* by McGraw-Hill was an instant best seller and has been transcribed into more than 20 languages. While his newest books it! and *Your Trajectory Code* released January 2015 by John Wiley, the world's largest trade book publisher, are best-sellers. *The Managerial-Leadership Bible, Revised Edition* his fourth college text book released also in 2015 by PEARSON EDUCATION, the world's largest academic text book publisher is changing how people look at human capital development and engagement!

His signature managerial-leadership engagement development series *THE LEADERSHIP ACADEMY OF EXCELLENCE* is utilized by many of the Fortune 100 firms, the ARMY National Guard, Federal Reserve, Farm Credit Banks, as well as Entrepreneurial business owners today at the C-Suite level and as an interactive engaged managerial-leadership effectiveness series with senior leaders. Understanding human capital performance and talent development, Jeff has a unique lens for revenue generation in everything he does and this is enhanced with his extensive sales training and coaching options for B2B and B2C utilization.

Recently, Magee was commissioned to design, train, and present a new series of national leadership and sales recruitment programs for more than the 5,000 professional sales recruiters and sales managers with the **U.S. Army National Guard.** For this he has subsequently received the prestigious **Commander's Coin of Excellence.** He also been invited to keynote at many major associations in America and at **West Point Military Academy** on leadership.

In 2010 while merging his business JEFF MAGEE INTERNATIONAL (Tulsa, OK) of 20 years with WesternCPE (Bozeman, MT), managing and developing a staff of more than 140 professionals, he steered a business from near financial collapse to significant profitability in a billion-dollar market segmentation.

MODULE ONE - Reinventing the Fundamentals of Managerial-Leadership Effectiveness: Performance Execution!®
By - Dr. Jeffrey Magee, CBE/CSP/CMC/PDM @ DrJeffSpeaks@aol.com
www.JeffreyMagee.com and www.ProfessionalPerformanceMagazine.com

Simultaneously Magee was recognized as **The U.S. Small Business Commerce Association (SBCA)** 2010 Best of Business Award in the Lecture bureau category. The SBCA Best of Business Award Program recognizes the best of small businesses throughout the country. Using consumer feedback and other research, the SBCA identifies companies that we believe have demonstrated what makes small businesses a vital part of the American economy. The selection committee chooses the award winners from nominees based off information taken from monthly surveys administered by the SBCA, a review of consumer rankings, and other consumer reports. Award winners are a valuable asset to their community and exemplify what makes small businesses great.

Over the past two decades leading training and development organizations such as Fred Pryor Seminars, SkillPath Seminars, CareerTrack Seminars, American Management Association, the Conference Board, AICPA, and Fortune 100 training enterprises have contracted with Magee to design courseware for them and provide train-the-trainer programs to equip others with his technologies to lead countless others to performance excellence around the World.

In 2011 Magee un-merged from WesternCPE to continue with his own firm *JeffreyMagee.com* (*Leadership Training & Technology/What You Need To Succeed!*), and has been a regular content provider to FCCServices, Farm Credit, AICPA, WesternCPE, iShade, CPELink, ARMY National Guard and many of the Fortune 500 Firms and Government Agencies, as well as appearing regularly at major conventions and Association conferences around the World. Twice invited to Keynote at the World Congress (Cannes, France and Vienna, Austria), Jeff is known to many as the "thought leaders, thought leader"!

With more than 200 hours of accredited CPE/CLE courseware and consulting deliverables for CPAs, EAs and Attorney's, Jeff has worked with and trained some of America's leading Subject-Matter-Experts (SMEs) within America's top consulting, accounting and legal organizations!

The London Business Gazette has hailed Jeff as "An American Business Guru." Recipient of the prestigious United States Junior Chamber of Commerce's "Ten Outstanding Young Americans" (TOYA) Award, former President George Bush and the U.S. Army National Guard recognized him with the high honor of the **"Total Team Victory & Freedom Award."** However, more important than Magee's credentials and accomplishments, he is market proven and here today to serve you.

Below is a link ... **FORBES** Does Feature Article on Jeffrey Magee (Las Vegas, Nevada): LINK and, LINK2 and, LINK3

TO BOOK JEFF - Jeff can be scheduled for your next Conference, Convention, Retreat, and Consulting or for an On-Site high impact results driven development program by contacting: DrJeffSpeaks@aol.com or by calling 406-548-5385.

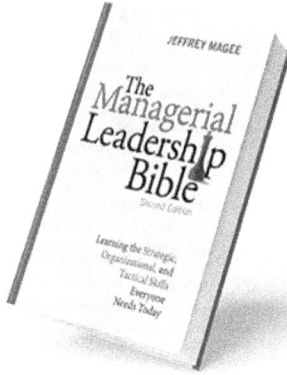

MODULE ONE - Reinventing the Fundamentals of Managerial-Leadership Effectiveness: Performance Execution!®
By - Dr. Jeffrey Magee, CBE/CSP/CMC/PDM @ DrJeffSpeaks@aol.com
www.JeffreyMagee.com and www.ProfessionalPerformanceMagazine.com

How I Can Serve You Next

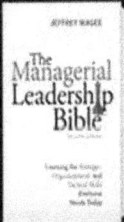

www.ingramcontent.com/pod-product-compliance
Lightning Source LLC
Chambersburg PA
CBHW050454190326
41458CB00005B/1283